The
Breast Cancer
Survivor's
Fitness Plan

Also by These Authors

Living Through Breast Cancer, by Carolyn M. Kaelin, M.D., M.P.H., with Francesca Coltrera

The Breast Cancer Survivor's Guide to Fitness (DVD), by Carolyn M. Kaelin, M.D., M.P.H., Josie G. Gardiner, and Joy Prouty

Also from Harvard Medical School

Beating Diabetes, by David M. Nathan, M.D., and Linda Delahanty, M.S., RD

Eat, Play, and Be Healthy, by W. Allan Walker, M.D., with Courtney Humphries

The Harvard Medical School Guide to Healthy Eating During Pregnancy, by W. Allan Walker, M.D., with Courtney Humphries

The No Sweat Exercise Plan, by Harvey B. Simon, M.D.

The Harvard Medical School Guide to Achieving Optimal Memory, by Aaron P. Nelson, Ph.D., with Susan Gilbert

The Harvard Medical School Guide to Lowering Your Cholesterol, by Mason W. Freeman, M.D., with Christine Junge

The Harvard Medical School Guide to Healing Your Sinuses, by Ralph B. Metson, M.D., with Steven Mardon

The Harvard Medical School Guide to Overcoming Thyroid Problems, by Jeffrey R. Garber, M.D., with Sandra Sardella White

The Harvard Medical School Guide to Lowering Your Blood Pressure, by Aggie Casey, R.N., M.S., and Herbert Benson, M.D., with Brian O'Neill

The Harvard Medical School Guide to a Good Night's Sleep by Lawrence Epstein, M.D., and Steven Mardon

Monthly Newsletters from Harvard Medical School

Harvard Health Letter
Harvard Women's Health Watch
Harvard Men's Health Watch
Harvard Heart Letter
Harvard Mental Health Letter

For more information, please visit us at health.harvard.edu.

The
Breast Cancer
Survivor's
Fitness Plan

Reclaim Health, Regain Strength, Live Longer

CAROLYN M. KAELIN, M.D., M.P.H.

FRANCESCA COLTRERA, JOSIE GARDINER, AND JOY PROUTY

McGraw·Hill

New York   Chicago   San Francisco   Lisbon   London   Madrid   Mexico City
Milan   New Delhi   San Juan   Seoul   Singapore   Sydney   Toronto

Library of Congress Cataloging-in-Publication Data

The breast cancer survivors fitness plan : reclaim health, regain strength, live longer /
    Carolyn M. Kaelin . . . [et al.].
         p.   cm.
     Includes index.
     ISBN 0-07-146578-2
     1. Breast—Cancer—Popular works.   I. Kaelin, Carolyn M.

  RC280.B8B6889   2007
  616.99'449—dc22   2006022311

1 2 3 4 5 6 7 8 9 0   DOC/DOC   0 9 8 7 6

ISBN-13: 978-0-07-146578-6
ISBN-10:   0-07-146578-2

Interior design by Think Design Group
Illustrations by Doron Ben-Ami

McGraw-Hill books are available at special quantity discounts to use as premiums and
sales promotions, or for use in corporate training programs. For more information, please
write to the Director of Special Sales, Professional Publishing, McGraw-Hill, Two Penn
Plaza, New York, NY 10121-2298. Or contact your local bookstore.

The information contained in this book is intended to provide helpful and informative
material on the subject addressed. It is not intended to serve as a replacement for
professional medical or fitness advice. Any use of the information in this book is at the
reader's discretion. The author, publisher, and the President and Fellows of Harvard
College specifically disclaim any and all liability arising directly or indirectly from the use
or application of any information contained in this book. A health care professional should
be consulted regarding your specific situation.

This book is printed on acid-free paper.

Contents

Preface

This book first began taking shape more than five years ago, when Josie Gardiner and Joy Prouty, two talented Reebok Master Trainers and longtime collaborators, began to develop an exercise program for breast cancer survivors. Just two years earlier, Josie had been through her own arduous treatments for uterine cancer. "At the end of my treatment," she recalls, "I weighed 100 pounds and could barely dry my own hair. I felt afraid, frail, and weak. I asked my doctor, 'What do I do now?'

" 'You're the master trainer,' he told me. 'You're the expert here. You know the answers better than I do.' "

This was true, Josie realized. Taking her own advice on exercise, she slowly but surely returned to the athletic life she loved. Yet the experience left her wondering about women in similar circumstances who did not have her specialized knowledge and abilities. Who was guiding their return to good health?

When Josie and Joy searched for a doctor who could bring a complementary set of skills to their project, breast cancer surgeon Carolyn Kaelin, M.D., M.P.H., FACS, the founding director of the Comprehensive Breast Health Center at Brigham and Women's Hospital in Boston, seemed the natural match. A leading national expert on breast cancer, Dr. Kaelin was well aware of the exhaustion and lingering discomforts reported by many of her patients long after their treatments had ended. She had collaborated on research designed to look closely at how exercise affects breast cancer survivors. One study, funded by the Lance Armstrong Foundation with Dr. Kaelin as the principal investigator, focused on rowing, a sport that involves repetitive arm movements. Ironically, Dr. Kaelin, too, would gain many insights into life on the other side of the stethoscope when she discovered her own breast cancer not long afterward.

Coming Together

Our combined talents were then distilled into four programs tailored to the specific needs of breast cancer survivors, which differ greatly depending on surgeries, treatments, and a multitude of other factors. At Fitcorp in Boston's Back Bay, we successfully worked with numerous breast cancer patients for over a year. Along with experts from the American College of Sports Medicine and Reebok University, we created a DVD called *The Breast Cancer Survivor's Guide to Fitness*. The responses we received to the DVD were enthusiastic and frequently came coupled with requests for a companion book. When *Living through Breast Cancer* was published in 2005, many women who read this comprehensive guide through the maze of breast cancer treatment and recovery wished for an expansion of the chapter on exercise. Thus, with the able assistance of Francesca Coltrera, an exceptional health writer and coauthor with Dr. Kaelin of *Living Through Breast Cancer*, this book was born. Throughout its pages, our intention is to offer workable solutions to many of the challenges faced by women after breast cancer treatments and reconstructive surgeries.

Acknowledgments

We were fortunate to be able to draw upon the considerable expertise of many people to help make these pages shine. While any errors or omissions are our responsibility, we gratefully acknowledge those who so generously shared their valuable expertise and time. Especially heroic efforts were made by quite a few. At Brigham and Women's Hospital, plastic surgeon Charles A. Hergrueter, M.D., an artful master of breast reconstruction, helped enormously. So, too, did Stacy Kennedy, M.P.H., RD/LDN, at Dana-Farber Cancer Institute and Anne Buckley, P.T., both of whom fielded even last-minute queries with aplomb. Sanaz Ghazal deserves our great appreciation for her part in building sturdy scaffolding for the DVD and the book. At Sports and Physical Therapy, Scott Waugh, P.T., ATC, director of rehabilitation for the Boston Red Sox (2004 World Champions!) and the Boston Bruins, patiently answered our many questions. Cedric X. Bryant, Ph.D., FACSM, chief exercise physiologist and the vice president of educational services at the American Council on Exercise, interrupted a well-deserved vacation to offer us invaluable input into our program.

We also wish to thank Walter C. Willett, M.D., Dr. P.H., chair of the Department of Nutrition at the Harvard School of Public Health, for the nutritional information provided in this book. Much appreciation likewise is due to Meryl S. Leboff, M.D., director of the Skeletal Health and Osteoporosis Center and Bone Density Unit, and Kenneth Baughman, M.D., director of the Advanced Heart Disease Section, both at Brigham and Women's Hospital, who provided articles and answered queries. Larry Raymond, Dr. Kaelin's unwaveringly helpful research assistant at Brigham and Women's Hospital, spent hours in the stacks at Harvard's Countway Medical Library and perched in front of a computer digging out much-needed information.

Others who kindly shared their fields of expertise include Bonnie Lasinski, P.T., CLT-LANA, Nancy J. Roberge, P.T., D.P.T., M.Ed., and Regina Kmet Schulman, LCMT, NCBTMB, CDT/ MLD. All three have worked to improve the lives of breast cancer survivors. Sally Edwards, a professional athlete and the author of several exercise books, has done so, too, as the cofounder of Team Survivor.

The Breast Cancer Survivor's Guide to Fitness DVD is both a companion to this book and its precursor, so it seems fitting to thank the wonderful team that brought the DVD to fruition. It was filmed at Reebok International in Canton, Massachusetts. There, Stephanie Montgomery, the director of Reebok University, helped us in so many ways, and Kathy O'Connell, vice president of fitness marketing at Reebok, and Annette Lang, LLC, Reebok Master Trainer, brought their significant talents to bear. Our very special thanks and appreciation also to Gray Cook, M.S., P.T., OCS, CSCS, the owner and director of Orthopedic and Sports Physical Therapy in Danville, Virginia. At Arnold Worldwide, we would like to thank Ron Lawner, chief creative officer, Lára T. Gislason, D. Scott Ferguson, and Allison K. Waters for their fine work on the DVD cover. Mark Hoffman, president at Dynamix, saw that the DVD made it out of the warehouse and onto the shelves. Hill-Holiday Interactive put great efforts into the DVD animations, which were artistically rendered by Raoul Kim. We also owe a debt of gratitude to Holly Metcalf, founder and director of the Row as One Institute, whose work contributed so much to the DVD as well as to this book. Shannon Ames, formerly director of operations and development at the Row as One Institute, coordinated every last detail and made sure all the work on the DVD moved along smoothly, too.

Every Friday afternoon for over a year we went to Fitcorp, a gleaming exercise facility in Boston, to meet with women recovering from breast cancer treatment while devising these programs for the DVD. We wish to particularly thank President and C.E.O Gary T. Klencheski and Mark Milligan, general manager for Fitcorp at the Prudential Center in Boston. Finally, we offer a very special round of thanks to the six ever-so-fabulous women who shared their experiences on the DVD and worked with us to show viewers exactly how the exercises should be done.

Many talented folks at McGraw-Hill and Harvard Health Publications have worked hard on this book. We owe a great deal to them all and would like to single out several for special appreciation. Our editor, Judith McCarthy, once again championed this project and guided us through it. Marisa L'Heureux, manager of editing, design, and production at the McGraw-Hill Professional division, listened with an open mind to our design requests and found a team to fulfill them. Dr. Anthony Komaroff, editor-in-chief of Harvard Health Publications, nurtured this book and helped us in many ways to move ahead with it. Assistant editor Raquel A. Schott put an enormous amount of effort into finding and working with excellent illustrators and keeping project details on track.

Steve Marsel, a photographer in Boston who has lent his remarkable vision to worthy causes like the Pan-Mass Challenge, which raises money for cancer research, photographed the outstanding cover for this book. Our book benefited, too, from a talented group of illustrators whose artwork appears in these pages. Raoul Kim, an animator whose illustrations appear on the DVD as well as in this book, and medical illustrators Harriet B. Greenfield and Scott Leighton did superb work.

For Doron Ben-Ami, who illustrated all of the exercises, we have the highest admiration. While his extraordinary talent speaks for itself, his patience and willingness to go many extra miles advanced this work immensely. Thank you so very much, Doron.

This book has given all of us many gifts. Among them are conversations with the wonderful women quoted inside its covers, who shared their experiences and challenges with warmth, grit, and grace. Their stories infuse much positive energy into these pages. It's our hope that this exercise program will do the same for them and for many thousands of others who share their circumstances. And, finally, a special salute to all who, along with Billy Starr, coordinator of the Pan-Mass Challenge bike ride, harness the good spirit of exercise to raise funds for worthy health-related causes.

The
Breast Cancer
Survivor's
Fitness Plan

CHAPTER 1

Taking Control

More than two million women living in the United States today have been treated for breast cancer, according to the American Cancer Society. Fortunately, we live at a time in medical history when increasingly sophisticated, lifesaving treatments are changing the course of this disease for hundreds of thousands of women. Just a handful of years ago, some of the most remarkable advances in surgery, radiation, and anticancer drugs were not yet widely available. Now, for most women, a breast cancer diagnosis may prove in hindsight to be a rough bump in the road, while the length of that road ultimately remains unchanged. For those living with metastatic breast cancer, an expanding list of treatments may be life-extending, also.

Yet whether breast cancer treatments have been tested over decades or emerge as new stars, they may take a heavy toll on a woman's body. "In barely a year, I've aged a decade," one breast cancer survivor succinctly reported, ticking off unwanted side effects of treatments that pile on pounds and weaken muscles and bones. Surgery to reconstruct the breast, which many women find life-enhancing, often presents additional challenges.

Now a growing body of research strongly suggests engaging in exercise reduces your risk for a recurrence and boosts the likelihood of living a longer, healthier life. What's more, a well-conceived, comprehensive exercise program can help you minimize or avoid many other concerns that arise after breast cancer treatments and reconstructive surgery.

No matter how uncomfortable or weak you might feel today, the simple, safe, and powerful program described in this book can help restore ease of movement and the strength and energy for daily tasks and pleasurable activities. Our goal is to enable you to rise to the joys and challenges each day brings. In essence, we hope to help you turn back the hands of a clock that spun forward far too quickly.

Laying the Foundation

Much of our program revolves around a series of progressive workouts. Yet safely and slowly stepping up your activities is only one part of your overall goal. Three other cornerstones of the program are a healthy diet, rest, and stress relief. What does this quartet have in common? Unlike so many aspects of breast cancer treatment, all four lie largely within *your* control. Together, they can significantly improve your health and the quality of your daily life. What's more, they can help you regain a sense of control over your own life that a cancer diagnosis so often undermines.

In the following sections, key facts and strategies are outlined. More in-depth information on paring off pounds, rebuilding muscle, and shoring up bones appears in Chapter 2.

Why Exercise?

In a nutshell, exercising regularly can help you:

- **Optimize longevity.** Being active cuts down the likelihood of breast cancer recurrence and boosts the odds of living longer. The long-term Nurses' Health Study surveys more than 120,000 female registered nurses about lifestyle factors and chronic diseases every two years. In 2005, researchers reporting on data drawn from nearly 3,000 study participants diagnosed with breast cancer found that those who engaged in even modest physical activity (such as walking for three to five hours over the course of a week) lessened the likelihood of recurrence and improved survival when compared with those who were sedentary or less active.

- **Gain energy.** One common concern stemming from breast cancer treatments is fatigue. Often, women report that their energy fluctuates day to day during treatment. Afterward, some women find energy returns fairly quickly, while others remain at low ebb for many months or longer. Slowly rebuilding endurance through easy cardiovascular exercise can help. According to the National Cancer Institute, some small, preliminary studies suggest that light to moderate walking or other activities may boost energy.

- **Improve mobility.** Discomforts that stem from mastectomy, lumpectomy, or lymph node surgery, radiation, and reconstructive surgery sometimes may be quite long-lasting, as Clara Walton can attest. Ever since her mastectomy and reconstructive surgery, her limited *range of motion*—that is, how far and in what directions someone can comfortably extend her arms, let's say, or turn her body easily—has bothered her. Nine years into survivorship, she says, she still hasn't recovered entirely. On a scale of 1 to 10, with 10 being the movement she had before her treatment began, she rated her ability to move easily and comfortably the first year after her surgeries at 3 or 4. Now, she says, it's closer to a 6 or 7. "Range of motion is still a problem," she notes.

    What causes this? Tightness created by scar tissue after surgery, radiation, moving muscle and tissue during reconstructive surgery, or simply disuse can limit your range of motion. Tightness also can lead to poor posture, which may contribute to other problems like an aching back. Over time, careful stretching expands a limited range of motion and helps release tightness.

- **Rebuild muscle and regain strength.** *Sarcopenia* is a simultaneous loss of muscle and gain in fat tissue. Aging, inactivity, chemotherapy, menopause, and possibly other hormonal changes brought on by breast cancer treatments all may cause muscle to dwindle while fat tissue builds up. Typically, excess weight accumulates as well. Exercise helps pare off unwanted pounds and rebuild muscle. Tipping the fat-muscle ratio of your body more favorably in the direction of muscle helps reverse losses in muscle and gains in fat that frequently occur during chemotherapy. Fat cells release estrogen, which fuels some breast cancers, and excess weight is associated with higher mortality in women who have had breast cancer.

Moving muscles during reconstructive surgery—a latissimus dorsi flap, for example, uses a large back muscle to re-create the breast—affects strength. Your body is quite practical, however, and often can use other muscles to help compensate for those no longer in their original place. Strengthening the appropriate compensating muscles helps ensure that you will be able to perform simple tasks like closing the hatchback or trunk of a car or lifting heavy groceries and comfortably engage in enjoyable activities such as cross-country skiing or tennis. Strength training also addresses muscle imbalances, which affect posture in ways that can spell future pain.

- **Keep bones healthy.** Research suggests that chemotherapy may speed bone loss in premenopausal women. In a Harvard study detailed in Chapter 2, researchers have found that within one year after beginning chemotherapy, particularly if chemotherapy induces premature menopause, a woman can lose 7 percent of the bone mass from her spine and 4 percent from her hips. For a woman going through natural menopause, this amount of bone loss usually takes five years to occur. Weight-bearing exercise, such as walking and strength training, coupled with calcium and vitamin D supplements as well as bone-saving medication, when appropriate, helps preserve bone.
- **Quell treatment-related nausea.** Some research shows that exercise may lessen nausea during chemotherapy, which will certainly improve your quality of life.
- **Enhance appearance.** Often, changes stemming from treatment undermine appearance and self-esteem. A 40-year-old woman undergoing chemotherapy commonly experiences a

Special Situations: When Exercise Is Especially Difficult

If you have compounding health conditions or disabilities, some of the exercises described in this book may be difficult or impossible for you to do. Sometimes even medications that improve your health may interfere with exercise to a lesser or greater degree. Kaelyn McGregor, a lively 42-year-old who has always been active, found that true this past year when she began taking a drug designed to combat metastases. "I've been dealing with a number of new physical challenges. I can assure you that trying to stay fit while also using a cane on certain days is quite the predicament," she says wryly. An experienced physical therapist or personal trainer may be able to suggest modifications of our exercises or an entirely different exercise plan tailored to your needs. Information on locating these professionals appears later in this chapter.

2.5 percent increase in body fat in one year. That's the equivalent of what typically occurs over 10 years to a 40-year-old without breast cancer. Exercise—which tones muscles and trims fat—helps turn back that clock.

- **Net additional health benefits.** Performed regularly, exercise tunes up the heart and lungs, eases insomnia and mild depression, boosts self-esteem, reduces high blood pressure and high cholesterol, and helps ward off many health conditions that shorten lives, including diabetes, colon cancer, heart disease, and stroke. On the other hand, being inactive is a risk factor for nearly all of these health concerns. When you realize that the majority of women who have had breast cancer will outlive their diagnosis and die one day of another cause entirely, it's easy to see how important staying active is for all of us.

Why Eat Well?

Eating well gives your body the energy and nutrients needed for healing, a process that continues after treatment ends. Protein, for example, is a building block used in the new cells that replace those lost to chemotherapy and radiation. Protein is necessary, too, during the cycles of regeneration and remodeling that take place in the skin after surgery. Countless other nutrients found in food play roles in healing as well. Vitamin C, vitamin A, zinc, and carbohydrates, fats, and fatty acids are a few examples.

Nutrients that help strengthen bones include calcium, vitamin D, vitamin K, magnesium, and phosphorus, which are found in food and available also through a daily multivitamin and supplements combining calcium and vitamin D. According to the National Osteoporosis Foundation, *osteoporosis*—a condition in which bone density thins out, leaving bones increasingly brittle and thus more likely to fracture—affects an estimated eight million women. As explained briefly in the preceding section as well as later in Chapter 2, research suggests the loss of bone mass that leads to osteoporosis may be hastened in women who experience menopause induced by chemotherapy. One study suggests chemotherapy may accelerate bone loss even when it does not prompt early menopause.

The foods you choose may have many other healthful nutrients. Filling much of your plate each day with a variety of colorful, pungent vegetables and fruits ensures you of a good supply of *antioxidants*, a catchall term for any compound that can counteract unstable molecules like free radicals, which are thought to have a hand in cancer, heart disease, and many other ailments. Paired with these antioxidants are countless other helpful nutrients that are not found in bottled supplements.

What about news reports that dietary fat may play a role in breast cancer recurrence? In 2005, researchers delving into this question through the large-scale Women's Intervention Nutrition Study (WINS) found that breast cancer recurred less frequently in those who consistently ate a low-fat diet. It is important to note that study participants who successfully stuck with the low-fat diet lost weight (roughly five pounds) and sustained this weight loss over the five years of the study. By contrast, during breast cancer treatment, most women gain weight. Many scientists speculate that it was the ability of WINS participants in the low-fat group to achieve and maintain a more healthy weight that led to fewer breast cancer relapses. Of course, a decrease in dietary fat and the substitution of fat calories with calories from fruits and vegetables may have played a role, too.

Currently, there is no other scientific evidence that even the healthiest diet will minimize the odds that breast cancer might recur. Possibly research will one day show this. Meantime, a varied diet that emphasizes vegetables, fruits, whole grains, beans and legumes, fish, poultry, and healthful oils (see Figure 1.1) does offer breast cancer survivors many important benefits by helping to ward off a variety of other cancers, diabetes, and cardiovascular ailments like heart attacks and strokes, among other illnesses.

What's more, loading up on vegetables and fruits can help crowd out less healthy foods—foods that often are higher in calories—simply because you'll be too full to eat them. That can help you reach or remain within a healthy weight range, which does appear to boost survival odds and lower recurrence rates among women who have had breast cancer. (See Chapter 2 for a full discussion of body mass index and healthy weight ranges.)

These tips can help you set yourself up to succeed:

- **Make healthy foods available.** Clear less healthy options out of your cabinets and refrigerator and restock regularly with healthy choices. Try to have quick, easy foods such as sliced vegetables on hand. Paying extra for shopping the salad bar or buying baby carrots may be worthwhile if you lack the time or energy to prepare foods.
- **At the grocery store, read labels carefully and make trade-offs that net you fewer calories and healthier fats.** Emphasizing foods that deliver relatively few calories per mouthful—romaine lettuce or carrots, for example, versus sirloin steak, cheese, or nuts—tends to fill you up faster at the table while cutting down calories, too.
- **Eat mindfully.** Truly taste your food and enjoy texture, scent, and visual pleasures rather than hurrying through a meal or nibbling while reading or watching TV. Slowing down as you eat helps in another way, too. The hormones in your gut that are responsible for signaling *satiety*—the news flash that announces that you've eaten enough—take about

FIGURE 1.1 The Harvard Healthy Eating Pyramid

The widest parts of the pyramid showcase the most important categories. Foods at the top should be eaten sparingly. Thus, daily exercise, weight control, healthy supplements, whole grains, vegetables, and fruits are housed in the wide base, while red meat, butter, sweets, and foods made with refined grains are at the narrow peak.

Adapted for breast cancer survivors from *Eat, Drink, and Be Healthy* by Walter C. Willett, M.D., and P. J. Skerrett.

20 minutes to deliver the message to your brain. Once that happens, you'll feel full.

- **Don't confuse thirst for hunger.** The thirst mechanism in humans is not well developed, and signals for both thirst and hunger originate in the same area in the brain, the hypothalamus. Often it is hydration our bodies crave, rather than calories. Keep on hand a glass of plain water, low-calorie flavored water, tea, or V8 juice. Phosphorous bubbles in carbonated beverages may leach calcium from the bones, so drink carbonated beverages in moderation.

- **Tune in to emotional cravings that can trip off overeating and have a plan in place for moments when emotional hunger strikes.** Turning to connections that

Do You Need Supplements?

An ever-lengthening list of supplements claims to cure whatever ails you or promises to tune up a sluggish immune response. Very little solid evidence backs such claims. A healthy diet supplies almost all the nutrients you need, and a basic multivitamin can fill in chinks. Usually, a calcium supplement paired with vitamin D is recommended, too (see Chapter 2 for amounts). Currently, the National Cancer Institute notes that no scientific evidence shows that vitamin or mineral supplements or herbal remedies can cure cancer or keep it from recurring. Some data suggest that 800 IU of vitamin D may help block certain cancers. Although that's higher than the normally recommended 200 IU to 600 IU of vitamin D depending on age, it is within safe limits.

If you do take any supplements or herbal remedies, tell your doctor and pharmacist so that potentially worrisome drug interactions can be considered. Many experts, for example, suggest erring on the side of caution by avoiding antioxidant supplements during radiation and chemotherapy, two treatments that harness oxidation to destroy cancer cells. It's also wise to remember that too much of a normally helpful nutrient—such as vitamin A or zinc, which is one of the *trace minerals* because your body needs very little to run efficiently—can be harmful. You're much less likely to get too much of specific nutrients through food.

make you feel happy, vital, and loved—whether family, friends, a partner, a pet, meditation, meaningful work, creative efforts, or enjoyable pursuits—may be an engaging substitute for unnecessary calories that affect your health as a breast cancer survivor. A quick walk or a few exercises often helps. A change in activities offers a distraction that can take your mind off food.

Why Rest?

The hours you spend sleeping appear to offer even more than a much-needed rest. While the links forged are still tentative, one sleep study that followed nearly 500 young adults for 13 years found that those who got the least sleep were apt to gain the most weight over time, although this association trailed off after age 34. Another much smaller study suggests insufficient sleep may tamper with levels of two appetite-regulating hormones: leptin, which suppresses hunger, and ghrelin, which enhances it. When sleep was deliberately curtailed, leptin levels dipped, ghrelin levels rose, and participants reported feeling hungry.

Burrowing beneath the covers for a sound night's sleep might have other benefits, too. Emerging evidence suggests that the hormone melatonin helps to spur production of certain immune cells and slow breast cancer cell growth. Nighttime darkness—for example, a bedroom with lights off and no flickering TV or glimmering streetlamp light—signals the pineal gland in the brain to churn out melatonin. Exposure to light during nighttime hours lessens the amount of melatonin released. Because some research suggests that the risk of developing breast cancer rises when melatonin levels are suppressed over the course of decades, it's worth speculating, as some experts do, that sleeping in a dark room every night may be one more way to reduce breast cancer risk. Support for this theory comes from the long-term Nurses' Health Study data published in 2006, which showed that nurses who routinely worked the night shift for 20 years or longer had a higher rate of breast cancer than those who worked during the day. Similar findings have occurred in other studies comparing female night-shift and day-shift workers and in research correlating morning melatonin levels to breast cancer risk.

One side effect of breast cancer treatments like surgery, chemotherapy, and radiation is that your body channels a great deal of energy into repairing or replacing damaged cells. Certain chemotherapy drugs temporarily suppress red blood cell production. Since red blood cells carry oxygen to cells throughout the body, this prompts anemia, which causes a fatigue that lifts gradually as the red blood cell count rebounds. Yet as treatment proceeds, exhaustion may snowball, especially if you have several types of treatment.

Not surprisingly, that can leave you feeling wiped out, as Dr. Kaelin found in the course of her own chemotherapy. "During my medical training—and particularly during my five-year surgical residency when I often was on call every other night—I became well accustomed to working through fatigue. Prior to being treated for breast cancer, six to seven hours of sleep left me well rested," she notes.

Yet while receiving chemotherapy and for months afterward, exhaustion prompted her to sleep nearly twice that long at night and sometimes nap during the day, too. "Even after sleeping deeply for 14 hours straight, I would wake up feeling fuzzy-headed, lethargic, and not refreshed. It took months before I started feeling like myself again."

Sometimes fatigue is tied to specific health issues, such as persistent anemia, medications, poor nutrition, depression, or a thyroid disorder called hypothyroidism. That's why it's important to tell your doctor about fatigue, especially if it is long-lasting. She or he can consider whether medications or a health problem might be the underlying cause.

Generally, experts believe it's wisest to give in to your body and get the rest you need right now. Removing the most obvious roadblocks to a good night's sleep will help. Sleep can be derailed for many reasons, so consider which of the following solutions and strategies apply to you:

- **Ease hot flashes.** Hot flashes triggered by anticancer drugs may wake you repeatedly during the night. Speak with your doctor about options. Nonmedical options include keeping a diary of hot-flash triggers such as alcohol, caffeine, or spicy foods and avoiding them; waiting a while until your body adjusts to medications; and engaging in relaxation therapy, which has been found to help ease hot flashes somewhat when done daily (see sidebar "Really Relaxing"). Keep a fan, a cold water bottle, and a cool, damp washcloth at your bedside (plus a change of night clothes and perhaps a folded sheet you can slip beneath you if you experience drenching sweats).

    If necessary, discuss medications with your doctor. Possibilities include the antidepressants venlafaxine (Effexor), paroxetine (Paxil), and fluoxetine (Prozac). Venlafaxine is notable for having little impact on sex drive. A 2005 multicenter trial suggests that gabapentin (Neurontin), a medication usually prescribed to treat seizures, migraines, and restless leg syndrome, helps reduce hot flashes related to breast cancer treatments. More than 400 women with breast cancer who were experiencing at least two hot flashes a day were randomly assigned for two months to take either 900 milligrams (mg) of gabapentin daily, 300 mg of gabapentin daily, or a placebo (sugar pill). Hot flashes occurred less frequently and were less intense among those who received 900 mg of gabapentin compared to those who took 300 mg or a placebo. There was no difference with respect to 10 other symptoms, suggesting that gabapentin was well tolerated. Currently, no studies compare the effectiveness of gabapentin for hot flashes against other nonhormonal medications.

The high blood pressure medication clonidine (Catapres) is sometimes prescribed, although trials suggest that the relief gained does not outweigh possible side effects. Other nonhormonal medications less commonly prescribed include the anticancer drug megestrol acetate (Megace) and medroxyprogesterone (Depo-Provera), which is typically used for birth control.

Natural approaches to hot flashes, such as vitamin E, black cohosh, red clover, dong quai, and soy have largely failed to help much, according to available studies. With the exception of vitamin E and, possibly, black cohosh, these natural remedies are weak plant estrogens (*phytoestrogens*). The question of whether they might be harmful for women who have had breast cancer, which sometimes is fueled by estrogen, is currently unanswered.

- **Set the stage for sleep.** Smoking, caffeine, and alcohol can disrupt sleep, particularly when indulged in close to bedtime. So can late sessions of exercise, which can actually help you sleep if done earlier in the day. Rearrange your routine as needed and work on cutting out unhealthy habits like smoking.

- **Try to calm unsettling emotions.** Anxiety or depression can make it hard to sleep. Relaxation tapes and techniques like those described in this chapter or learning the steps for self-hypnosis may help. Counseling and, possibly, antianxiety or antidepression medications may be necessary, as well.
- **Practice good sleep habits.** Get up at the same time each day. Try ending naps before midafternoon and keeping them short. A light bedtime snack, but not a heavy meal, may make you sleepy. A pleasantly dark, quiet bedroom kept at a comfortable temperature encourages sleep. If you truly can't sleep, it may be best to curl up elsewhere to read a book, listen to calming music, or watch TV until you feel ready for bed. Finally, if all else fails to work, discuss sleep medications with your doctor.

Why Engage in Stress Relief?

Research suggests that stress suppresses the immune system. It has been proven to slow healing and also may make you more susceptible to some illnesses, such as the common cold. Chronic stress boosts blood pressure and the risk of heart disease. Relieving stress through relaxation techniques (see sidebar "Really Relaxing"), performed regularly, can ease or erase many of these effects.

Not surprisingly, a breast cancer diagnosis pushes you off balance emotionally and can send stress soaring. This feeds anxiety and depression, which usually wax and wane and tend to spike at certain flash points. The moment you heard your diagnosis may have been a terrible shock. Other times that may be especially difficult are waiting for a pathology report, the stretch between diagnosis and starting treatment, and treatment itself. While some women are utterly jubilant on their last day of active treatment, others find this a hard transition to make or run into trouble months afterward.

Finding your balance and lowering your stress level during and after treatment is essential for your well-being. Taking heed of the following can help:

- **Set aside relaxation time.** Making relaxation time a priority will help you rebalance and rejuvenate yourself. Dress in loose-fitting clothes and sit or lie in a comfortable position in a quiet spot to practice relaxation techniques. A classic method based upon the relaxation response described by Dr. Herbert Benson, a Harvard cardiologist well-known for his groundbreaking work on the link between mind and body, appears in the sidebar.
- **Think short and sweet.** Brief relaxation techniques are especially helpful at high-stress moments—during tests or treatment, when a hot flash strikes, or when a craving for less healthy pursuits arises. Breathe deeply, so that air fully fills your lungs and your lower abdomen rises slightly. Put your hand beneath your navel so you can feel the gentle rise and fall of your belly as you breathe. Breathe in slowly while silently counting to five. Breathe out slowly while silently counting to five. Continue for a minute or longer. Try these techniques while sitting or lying down comfortably or engage in deep breathing during a walk.
- **Try different options.** Listen to soft, meditative music. Let yourself drift in and out of the rhythm, swaying slightly to the music or simply feeling the beat. Or visualize yourself in a warm, welcoming place—at the beach, in the mountains, in a park—anyplace in the world where you feel relaxed enough to leave your worries behind for a while.
- **Carve out time to enjoy yourself.** See a movie, join friends for dinner, go dancing, curl up with a book, or explore new passions. Caring for yourself by indulging in enjoyable pursuits can be a great stress-buster.
- **Get the help you need.** If depression or anxiety is interfering with your daily life, supportive therapy or counseling, possibly along with antianxiety or antidepressant medication,

Really Relaxing

Landmark research done by Dr. Herbert Benson, a cardiologist at Harvard Medical School who founded the Mind/Body Institute in Boston, shows that regularly inducing a deep state of relaxation helps erase many effects of chronic stress. Tension, anxiety, and insomnia also may respond to this approach. Some women even find that relaxation techniques help cool hot flashes. A two-month study of women bothered by tamoxifen-induced hot flashes found that the group practicing relaxation daily had significantly fewer hot flashes than usual, while hot-flash intensity increased for a control group not trained in the relaxation technique. One step-by-step way to induce the relaxation response is:

1. **Choose a word, prayer, or phrase to help you focus.** Silently repeat this ("one," "peace," "Om," "breathing in calm"). Close your eyes if you like, or focus on an object in the room.

2. **Adopt a passive attitude.** Disregard distracting thoughts. Anytime your attention drifts, simply say, "Oh, well" to yourself and return to silently repeating your focus word or phrase.

3. **Slowly relax all of your muscles.** Move your attention gradually from your face down toward your feet, relaxing the muscle groups as you go. Breathe easily and naturally while using your chosen phrase for 10 to 20 minutes. After you finish, remain quiet for a minute or so with your eyes closed. If you are using the technique to help you fall asleep, allow yourself to drift off. Otherwise, open your eyes and continue to remain quiet for a minute before standing up.

4. **Practice daily to reap full health benefits or as needed to relax.** Try to meditate for 10 to 20 minutes or longer, preferably at the same time each day.

can do a great deal to help. Preferably, find a mental health professional who has worked with women who have had breast cancer. Your cancer care team or regular doctor may have suggestions, or you can contact the American Psychosocial Oncology Society (apos-society.org or 866-APOS-4-HELP) for a referral.

- **Seek support.** Consider joining a support group in person or online. Your cancer care team may be able to suggest one, or you can check with breast cancer organizations in your area (see Resources). A willing listener may help, too. Ask your most trusted friends or family if you can count on them to listen when you need to talk. That can make it easier to make a call or a connection at the time when you really need a shoulder. If religion is an anchor in your life, seek comfort and support from your religious or spiritual leader.

Creating a Team

Just as it took a team of dedicated professionals to coordinate all of your treatment, enlisting others will help enormously as you work with the exercises in this book. So, who's on your team and how can they help?

Your Health Care Team

When can you safely start the exercises in this book? While the timing we propose is conservative, it may not be best for you. Discuss the program with your surgeon, and with your oncologist, if you have one, with an eye toward finding out whether you need to start more slowly and whether there are any limits on what you can do. This is very important! You also should find out if any medications you take might affect you while exercising.

If you take medications unrelated to breast cancer, speak with the doctor who prescribed those. Beta-blockers, for example, are prescribed for high blood pressure, anxiety, and certain heart problems. They reduce your heart rate (how often your heart beats), which in turn can lower your blood pressure. After you exercise, veins in your body may become more dilated (wider) than usual, which causes a dip in blood pressure. Occasionally, veins remain dilated long enough in some people to cause dizziness or fainting. As veins contract back to their usual, smaller diameter, blood pressure rises and these symptoms disappear. If you experience lightheadedness, dizziness, or faintness, try slowing the pace of your workouts and increasing the cooldown time (see Chapter 9, Exercise with Care). If symptoms persist, tell your doctor, who may wish to adjust your medication.

Usually, it's safe to exercise no matter which medications you are taking. You simply need to be aware of symptoms that suggest you should slow down or stop.

A Physical Therapist

Particularly if you had reconstructive surgery, a mastectomy, or traditional lymph node surgery (see Chapter 3), a physical therapist is a vital member of your team. Seeing a physical therapist early can help you avoid trouble that compounds over time through disuse, muscle imbalances, and poor posture. Pain, tightness, and difficulty moving may interfere with normal muscle and joint function after all but the most minimal surgery. Other problems can stem from moving muscle, skin, and fat from the back or abdomen to the chest to form the new breast mound or pushing the chest muscle outward to create a pocket for an implant.

Physical therapists are trained to help people recover movement and function in any part of the body that has been affected by surgery, debilitating illness, or simply lack of use. Their training also enables them to work with people who have disabilities or health concerns such as heart ailments, osteoporosis, and arthritis, which add an additional level of complexity to recovery after breast cancer treatments. Their tools include massage to release tight muscles or tightness due to scar tissue, passive stretching to improve shoulder range of motion, and progressive exercises focused on gradually strengthening and balancing affected muscle groups. Usually, health insurance will pay for physical therapy sessions (sometimes this is true only if a specific problem is identified, rather than to prevent future problems). There may be a cap on the number of sessions per year.

When seeking out a physical therapist, ask about certification and expertise, which varies widely. Membership in a professional organization, such as the American Physical Therapy Association, is a good sign. Physical therapists must be college graduates and may have a master's degree (M.A.) or, less often, a doctorate (Ph.D.). They take a national exam and must be licensed in the state where they practice. The American Board of Physical Therapy Specialties certifies fields of advanced degree training, including specialties in women's health, sports, cardiopulmonary therapy, geriatrics, and orthopedics. A physical therapist experienced in working with women who have been treated for breast cancer can be especially helpful. Your cancer care team or hospital may be able to refer you to a physical therapist, or you can find one through word of mouth or by contacting the American Physical Therapy Association (apta.org or 800-999-2782).

A Personal Trainer

Even if weekly sessions with a personal trainer are beyond your price range, a few initial sessions can be very helpful. "An experienced trainer meets you at your starting point, whether you are a gifted athlete or rarely leave the couch, and then tailors a program and adjusts exercises to fit your needs," says Joy Prouty. "The trainer can show you how good form feels—that is, make sure you understand how to position yourself correctly and move through each exercise properly so that you can achieve the best results and avoid setting yourself up for injury. A good trainer also acts as a coach, a motivator, and a cheerleader." That can help enormously on days when you simply don't feel like exercising.

If you can only see a personal trainer a few times, the best time to start would be before launching into the program in this book. This offers you additional guidance in helping you perform the exercises correctly. The trainer can see if any modifications will be helpful and then follow your progress over the course of a few sessions.

Before choosing a personal trainer, inquire carefully about credentials. There is no national standard for personal trainers, so training, experience, and ability vary widely. Look for certification from a well-respected program, such as the American College of Sports Medicine (ACSM) or the American Council on Exercise (ACE). Other respected credentials include those from the National Council on Strength and Fitness (NCSF), National Strength and Conditioning Association (NSCA), and National Academy of Sports Medicine (NASM). Ask if the trainer has experience in working with women who have been treated for breast cancer and, especially, reconstructive surgery, if that applies to you. Sometimes your cancer care team, a local hospital or gym, or word of mouth from other women who have had breast cancer can help you find a good trainer.

A Massage Therapist

Professional massage helps relax muscles and soothe aches and pains. That may extend your range of motion and generally make you feel more comfortable. Massage is a great stress-reliever for many women and also can be a nice way to get back in touch—literally—with your body. Be sure to give the massage therapist feedback about which strokes and how much pressure feel good. After surgery, certain areas of your body where nerves were affected may feel numb or extra-sensitive to any touch.

There is no national standard for massage therapists, so training and expertise vary widely. It's wise to ask whether a massage therapist is licensed because some states do require this. Likewise, inquire about training, experience, and credentials. If possible, seek out a massage therapist who has additional education and expertise in working with people being treated for breast and other cancers. Two professional organizations that have established training criteria for massage therapy are the American Massage Therapy Association (AMTA) (amtamassage.org or 877-905-2700) and the National Certification Board for Therapeutic Massage and Bodywork (ncbtmb.com or 630-627-8000).

A Lymphedema Therapist

Lymphedema is a swelling in the arm or sometimes trunk of the body due to the backup of lymph, a protein-rich fluid containing water, fat, bacteria, and fragments of old blood cells. Lymphedema may occur after surgery or radiation alters lymphatic channels. A certified lymphedema therapist, who is trained in specific massage techniques called *manual lymphatic drainage* and comprehensive care known as *complete decongestive therapy* (*CDT*), can help relieve this condition. Your cancer care team or a hospital may be able to refer you to someone, or you can contact the National Lymphedema Network (lymphnet.org or 800-541-3259). See Chapter 3 for additional advice on finding a certified lymphedema therapist as well as current recommendations for reducing the risk of developing lymphedema and easing lymphedema when it does occur. Chapter 9 contains information on exercising safely if you are at risk for lymphedema or have experienced it.

Friends and Family

Enlisting others can pave the way for you to find the time to exercise and boost your resolve to do so. Ask your partner, spouse, family members, or friends to ensure you of a regular block of time by taking certain tasks off your plate. Perhaps someone in your circle can join you in walking or in other parts of your exercise program a few days a week. If you make a date, you'll be less likely to skip exercise and may find it more fun. Designate a friend to check up on whether you've been working out and to brainstorm with you about ways to remove any roadblocks. Likewise, ask those you live with to support you in eating well by helping to keep healthy foods well-stocked and less healthy choices at a minimum at home.

CHAPTER 2

Pounds, Muscles, and Bones

It is frustrating, yet true, that the very anticancer treatments that save lives can further compromise good health by affecting your weight, muscles, and bones. Chemotherapy, for example, often contributes to weight gain and *sarcopenia*, a simultaneous loss of muscle and rise in fat tissue. Some anticancer drugs also prompt swifter than normal loss of bone mass. Fortunately, you can actively work to remedy these unwanted changes. This chapter outlines three key health concerns—added weight, dwindling muscle, and thinning bones—raised by breast cancer treatments and presents workable solutions.

Paring Off Pounds

When at 33 Meg Reyes learned she had breast cancer, she decided to make a few changes. While she hadn't been terribly active, she started walking regularly. And by sticking to a sensible, somewhat strict diet, she lost 35 pounds. "I realize I'm the only person that can change my life," she notes simply. Research strongly suggests that Meg is moving in the right direction on all counts.

The Concerns

Go ahead. Tap three women on the shoulder. Odds are good that one or more has watched the scale creep up and quite possibly struggled to bring her weight back down. This very common health issue is especially problematic for breast cancer survivors. Studies show that up to 50 percent or more of women gain weight during chemotherapy, which may be compounded by hormonal changes, especially among women thrust into an early menopause. Usually, women put on 5 to 15 pounds, although greater gains are not uncommon. These gains add to fat stores, not muscle mass. A 40-year-old woman undergoing chemotherapy typically experiences a 2.5 percent boost in body fat in a single year—that's equivalent to what a healthy 40-year-old might expect to gain in a decade!

Certain factors make gaining weight more likely, including undergoing longer chemotherapy regimens; taking the steroid prednisone (a supportive medication used during chemotherapy to help quell certain side effects); receiving chemotherapy through pills rather than intravenous (IV) infusion; and being pre-menopausal or experiencing premature menopause. Many women also complain of gaining weight while on hormonal medications such as tamoxifen (Nolvadex). Currently no firm evidence pins these additional pounds on the medication, yet the bottom line—or rather, the needle on the scale—is that many women do gain weight.

Any treatment for breast cancer, whether it's surgery, radiation, or anticancer drugs, is likely to slow you down and make exercising and eating well much harder than usual. You may nibble more—certainly, women staving off noxious tastes and nausea linked to chemotherapy often do—and move around less. Perhaps healthy foods aren't as soothing or palatable as certain calorie-packed, less nutritious choices, or overall stress simply makes the effort to eat well too high a hurdle to jump. When she embarked on chemotherapy at age 36, Kaelyn McGregor, an active member of Young Survival Coalition, says that nutrition initially took a backseat to more comforting foods. "I said, '*I've got cancer.* I'm going to eat pizza and gummy bears! You can't stop me.' And everybody was on board with that." Later, she worked hard to lose some of the weight she had added.

Why is attaining or maintaining a healthy weight so important after breast cancer treatment?

- **The bottom line: improving survival.** Emerging research indicates that avoiding significant weight gain after diagnosis cuts recurrence rates and may improve survival, although the issue is quite complex. In 2005, researchers reporting on Nurses' Health Study data found that women who had never smoked and had gained an average of 17 pounds after breast cancer treatment had a greater than 50 percent increased risk of death or recurrence over the course of nine years compared to those who maintained their weight. Such a change in weight also was worrisome for two other groups: women diagnosed with early-stage cancers and women whose weight at diagnosis had been normal (a body mass index below 25). Previous research on women who had chemotherapy found that the risk of death was 60 percent higher among those who gained more than 12 pounds compared to those who gained less.

- **Decreasing circulating estrogen.** Parked on the surface of cells are molecules known as receptors that recognize hormones circulating in the bloodstream. One such molecule, the estrogen receptor, is found on the surface of cells in roughly 70 percent of breast cancer tumors. The hormone estrogen can fuel these breast cancers. Before menopause, estrogen produced by a woman's ovaries overwhelms estrogen from other sites in her body. After menopause, the ovaries stop churning out estrogen. Then the main source of estrogen becomes the enzyme *aromatase*, which exists primarily in our fat cells (adipose tissue) and helps convert other naturally occurring hormones into estrogen. Less adipose tissue equals less aromatase, and less aromatase means less circulating estrogen.

  In addition, when women stay within a normal weight range most of the estrogen circulating in the bloodstream is

Taking It Off on Taxes?

One of the newer tax deductions for medical expenses may improve your health while trimming your annual tax bill. Currently the Internal Revenue Service (IRS) allows you to deduct some expenses paid to lose weight. A doctor must specify that weight loss qualifies as treatment for a specific ailment, such as obesity, heart disease, or high blood pressure. While a gym or health club membership or a visit to a spa wouldn't be covered, membership and meeting fees for a weight loss group or separate fees for weight loss activities at your gym or health club would qualify. Under certain circumstances, part of the cost of special foods (not diet foods or items that meet normal nutritional needs) may qualify, too. Check with the IRS (see Topic 502-Medical and Dental Expenses at irs.gov or call 800-829-1040) or contact a tax specialist for requirements and specific information.

tied to a protein, such as sex hormone binding globulin (SHBG). Tethered this way, estrogen is not *bioavailable*, meaning that it cannot reach vulnerable cells that could be fueled by it. Overweight women have higher amounts of insulin and insulin-like growth factors, which decrease SHBG. The combination of higher estrogen production from fat cells and fewer available binding proteins is a double whammy.

- **Minimizing risk for lymphedema.** Excess weight raises the risk of lymphedema. Research suggests being obese— that is, having a BMI of 30 or higher (see "A Healthy Weight" sidebar)—puts you at significantly greater risk for developing lymphedema.
- **Outliving breast cancer, decreasing risks for other conditions.** Being overweight or obese (see "A Healthy Weight" sidebar) boosts the odds of developing a laundry list of serious ailments and possibly dying early. Among these are heart disease, diabetes, a variety of cancers, stroke, gallstones, and high blood pressure. Also, added pounds exacerbate arthritis and often affect self-esteem. Other health problems accrue, as well.

The Solutions

Whether you wish to keep the needle on your scale hovering at a healthy weight or need to pare off pounds to enhance your health, these tips can help you achieve success.

- **Balance calories in with calories out.** If you are within or beyond a healthy weight range (see sidebar), start by focusing on not adding pounds. To make that possible, daily calories from food and drink must equal calories expended through activity. Additional calories prompt weight gain; fewer calories trigger weight loss. If you need to lose weight, discuss with your doctor the best way for you to do so at this point in time. Sometimes it's best to wait. Dieting may not be a good idea during cancer treatments when your body needs protein, calories, and nutrients from a varied diet to heal and rebuild cells.

- **Eat thoughtfully.** The Harvard Healthy Eating Pyramid in Chapter 1 (see Figure 1.1) outlines an eating plan that enhances overall health. Tips for paring down extra calories and reaching or remaining at a healthy weight also appear there.

- **Start moving.** Cardiovascular exercise, such as walking, is the best form of activity to burn off calories. Our walking program, which starts off as slowly as necessary and builds up gradually, is described in Chapter 10. Try to carve out time for walking on as many days of the week as possible. Even walking for five minutes every hour will burn some calories. We know that energy fluctuates a great deal during treatment and recovery. Just do what you can day by day. Any activity is better than none.

Rebuilding Muscle

All of her life, Liz Usborne played sports. She swam frequently. She played basketball during college and later knocked tennis balls around the court two or three times a week. She volunteered as a referee for children's sports, a task that often calls for running up

A Healthy Weight

The health implications of weight reach well beyond any role it plays in breast cancer. According to researchers at the Harvard School of Public Health, three measures that help determine whether you fall within a healthy range are a ratio of height to weight known as *body mass index* (BMI), waist size, and the amount of weight gained since you turned 21.

Body Mass Index (BMI)

BMI offers a snapshot of total body fat for the average person, although the results can be thrown off if you are especially well muscled or well padded. On the chart (see Figure 2.1), a woman with a BMI of 25 through 29 is considered overweight; a woman with a BMI of 30 or higher is considered obese. A substantial number of studies drawing on data collected from more than a million adults shows that a BMI higher than 25 raises the risk for many illnesses, including cancers, heart disease, diabetes, and stroke. Although your fears may center on dying early from breast cancer, once your BMI goes above 25, the odds of shaving years off your life because of one of these other health problems rise, too.

Waist Circumference

Where pounds settle also may matter. Some studies suggest that abdominal fat contributes to high blood sugar, blood pressure, and cholesterol and has a hand in heart disease, too. (Of course, a thickening waist may just be a marker of overall fat rather than a unique form of fat.) Measure your waist at the point where your sides dip in or at belly-button height. According to the National Institutes of Health (NIH), a healthy waist measurement for women is less than 35 inches. Harvard researchers warn that this is a generous estimate. Beyond that, risk rises for diabetes, heart disease, high blood pressure, high cholesterol, and cancer.

Weight Gained

If you've gained more than 10 pounds since you turned 21, your health could profit from slimming down. Data from the Nurses' Health Study showed women who added 11 to 22 pounds in middle age were far more likely to develop heart disease, type 2 diabetes, gallstones, and high blood pressure than those who put on 5 pounds or less.

and down the sidelines. Yet after two breast cancer surgeries and six months of chemotherapy, during the course of which Liz became quite ill, the muscles that powered her days seemed to dissolve. "I was jelly," she says. "I had no muscles left." It took many

FIGURE 2.1 Body Mass Index (BMI) Chart

Your body mass index (BMI): Are you a healthy weight?													
Height	Weight in pounds												
4'10"	91	96	100	105	110	115	119	124	129	134	138	143	167	191
4'11"	94	99	104	109	114	119	124	128	133	138	143	148	173	198
5'0"	97	102	107	112	118	123	128	133	138	143	148	153	179	204
5'1"	100	106	111	116	122	127	132	137	143	148	153	158	185	211
5'2"	104	109	115	120	126	131	136	142	147	153	158	164	191	218
5'3"	107	113	118	124	130	135	141	146	152	158	163	169	197	225
5'4"	110	116	122	128	134	140	145	151	157	163	169	174	204	232
5'5"	114	120	126	132	138	144	150	156	162	168	174	180	210	240
5'6"	118	124	130	136	142	148	155	161	167	173	179	186	216	247
5'7"	121	127	134	140	146	153	159	166	172	178	185	191	223	255
5'8"	125	131	138	144	151	158	164	171	177	184	190	197	230	262
5'9"	128	135	142	149	155	162	169	176	182	189	196	203	236	270
5'10"	132	139	146	153	160	167	174	181	188	195	202	207	243	278
5'11"	136	143	150	157	165	172	179	186	193	200	208	215	250	286
6'0"	140	147	154	162	169	177	184	191	199	206	213	221	258	294
6'1"	144	151	159	166	174	182	189	197	204	212	219	227	265	302
6'2"	148	155	163	171	179	186	194	202	210	218	225	233	272	311
6'3"	152	160	168	176	184	192	200	208	216	224	232	240	279	319
6'4"	156	164	172	180	189	197	205	213	221	230	238	246	287	328
BMI	19	20	21	22	23	24	25	26	27	28	29	30	35	40
	HEALTHY WEIGHT						OVERWEIGHT					OBESE		

◻ Healthy weight 18.5–24 ▨ Overweight 25–29 ▨ Obese 30+

Directions: Weigh yourself without clothes and measure your height without shoes. Find your height at the left of the table. Follow across until you hit the box with your weight. Your BMI will be at the bottom of that column.

According to the World Health Organization, a BMI of 25 or more qualifies as overweight and 30 or more indicates obesity. A lean BMI (18.5 to 22) is best for health. As a realistic first step, shoot for the best weight you've maintained for a year after the age of 20. Remember, too, that any step in the right direction will be helpful.

Source: Report of the Dietary Guidelines Advisory Committee on the Dietary Guidelines for Americans, 2000.

months of workouts with a physical therapist before Liz could regain the strength and abilities she had lost.

The Concerns

Over time, muscle slips away year by year in all but the most active among us. Contrary to popular belief, muscle tissue never converts to fat, nor will fat ever change to muscle. Yet as muscle

FIGURE 2.2 Sarcopenia

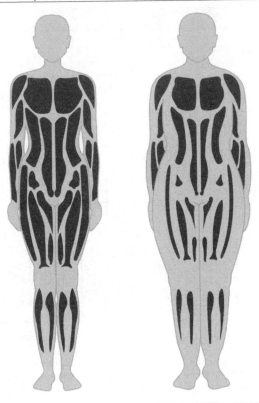

The simultaneous rise in fat tissue and dwindling of muscle tissue known as sarcopenia may be due to aging, menopause, chemotherapy, inactivity, or a combination of these and other factors.

dwindles, all other things being equal, a larger percentage of the body is made up of fat tissue.

Anticancer treatments can accelerate this process to a surprising degree. Chemotherapy may prompt an early, sometimes permanent, menopause. Sarcopenia—a simultaneous boost in fat tissue and loss of muscle tissue, particularly in large muscle groups such as the hips, buttocks, and thighs—typically follows (Figure 2.2). Sarcopenia also is seen around the time of menopause and as we age. It may stem from physical inactivity and a variety of medical conditions and medications, too.

A lack of activity, understandable when treatment and recovery sap energy, compounds the situation. A study published in the *Journal of Clinical Oncology* found that women were less active physically during the first year after diagnosis. Other research suggests that this slowdown can be tied to fatigue. It's wise to note that the shift in body composition—less muscle, more fat—occurs against the backdrop of a nationwide struggle with obesity, a health problem that only can be addressed by cutting down on calories and stepping up exercise.

Why are rebuilding muscle and losing fat tissue so important after breast cancer treatment?

- **Reduce an estrogen source.** A more favorable muscle-to-fat ratio helps reduce one source of estrogen, the enzyme aromatase that converts our natural low levels of male hormones into estrogen. This added estrogen, in turn, may encourage some breast cancer cells to multiply.
- **Lower circulating estrogens.** Activity itself appears to cut down on estrogens circulating in the bloodstream, too. One 2004 study randomly assigned previously sedentary, overweight women ages 50 to 75 to a group that exercised moderately for 45 minutes a day, five days a week or a group that did stretching exercises. After three months, researchers noted significant declines of three types of circulating estrogens in women who exercised. Declines continued—though not significantly—among the exercisers over the course of a year. Meanwhile, estrogen levels rose somewhat in those who simply stretched.
- **Rebuild strength and protect against falls.** Weakened muscles compromise your ability to engage in everyday tasks and enjoyable activities. They contribute to falls and thus, quite possibly, to fractures and loss of independence. The simplest motions—lifting packages, reaching overhead, rising from a chair—may tax your strength, depending upon how treatments and reconstructive surgery, if you had it, have affected you. Inactivity over the years plays into this problem. Research shows that the right exercise program can

reverse part, or in some cases nearly all, of these declines at any age.

- **Help burn calories.** Pound for pound, muscle burns a few more calories than fat. While muscle added through our walking and light-weight strength-training program may only shave off a handful of calories a day, even small differences can add up over time to help tip the scale to your benefit.
- **Tone muscles, enhance appearance.** Toned, strong muscles improve your appearance and abilities, which can be a nice boost to self-esteem laid low by breast cancer treatments.

The Solutions

While no magic or alchemy exists to turn fat into muscle, applying the tips that follow will help you pare away fat and strengthen muscles.

- **Shift your body composition.** A program of walking and strength training will gradually build muscle tissue and peel off fat tissue so that your muscle-to-fat ratio becomes more favorable.
- **Combine your efforts.** Half an hour of brisk walking burns nearly 150 calories. A few scoops of ice cream or a candy bar could replace each one and then some. The net result? No change in the muscle-to-fat ratio or worse, change in the wrong direction. Try not to undermine exercise success by rewarding yourself with calorie-laden treats. Whether you're trying to lose weight or change your muscle-to-fat ratio, stepping up exercise while cutting down calories works best.
- **Stay the course.** You didn't lose muscle overnight, and you won't rebuild it that way either. Commit to wellness by scheduling regular slots of time for exercise and following through on your exercise plan. See Chapter 10 for tips on building your routine.

Essential Muscles

A beating heart and a flexed bicep are hard-working muscles known to all of us. We would do well to become equally aware of a lesser-known set of internal muscles that act as a sling to help hold the bladder in place. Strengthening the *pubococcygeus* muscles assists in warding off or reversing *stress incontinence*, the leakage of urine prompted by a sneeze, a cough, a belly laugh, or similar stresses. Pregnancy, childbirth, hormonal changes due to menopause or to anticancer medications that lower estrogen levels, and aging are factors that may contribute to weakening of these muscles.

To locate the right muscles, experts at the National Institute of Diabetes and Digestive and Kidney Diseases suggest imagining using your vagina to suck in a small marble. Count to three as you pull the muscles upward.

Relax for a count of three and repeat. Work up to three sets of 10 repetitions a day. Daily practice for three to six weeks should net improvements. Since the sling of muscles is internal, you'll be able to do these exercises practically anytime. Try to fit them into your daily routine: before getting out of bed, while showering, while on hold on the phone or stuck in traffic, or at other convenient times.

At first, 10 repetitions may seem impossible, notes Wendy, who finds these exercises essential, especially after menopause. "Don't give up, though. I told myself, 'I'm just going to start with 5.'" As her muscles became stronger, doing more repetitions became easier. Sometimes it helps to do the exercises lying down, she adds, so that you aren't working as hard against gravity.

Shoring Up Bones

Throughout life, bones are continually built up by cells called *osteoblasts* and torn down by cells called *osteoclasts*, which are tasked with freeing up minerals like calcium stored in the bones for use elsewhere in the body. Generally, a woman builds 98 percent of her skeletal mass by age 20 and reaches *peak bone mass* by age 30. After that peak, osteoblasts fail to keep pace with osteoclasts, allowing bone loss to begin. Bones don't disappear, of course. Their structure just becomes increasingly lacy and thus weaker. Usually, this decline in bone density picks up speed around menopause when the ovaries stop pumping out estrogen,

FIGURE 2.3 Bone Changes in Osteoporosis

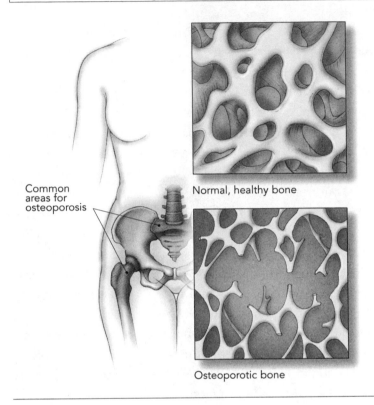

Common areas for osteoporosis

Normal, healthy bone

Osteoporotic bone

Osteoporosis, a condition that makes bones fragile and more likely to fracture, affects an estimated eight million women. The thinning of normal, healthy bone that may lead to osteoporosis accelerates at menopause. Chemotherapy appears to speed bone loss, too, particularly among women who experience early menopause due to it. Certain other anti-cancer drugs may play a role in bone thinning as well. The wrists, spine, and hips are the three most common sites for fractures, although any bone may be affected.

which helps protect bones. Eventually bone thinning can lead to *osteoporosis*, a condition that makes bones fragile and far more likely to fracture (Figure 2.3). The National Osteoporosis Foundation estimates that eight million women have osteoporosis and millions more have low bone mass (osteopenia), which puts them at higher risk for developing osteoporosis.

Fractures tied to osteoporosis are serious business. In women who have been treated for breast cancer, the wrist, spine, and hip are the most vulnerable sites, but any bone in the body may be affected. Aside from pain and immobility, two-thirds of those who break a bone because of osteoporosis never fully regain their previous level of functioning. Roughly one in four people over 50 will die in the year following a hip fracture, often from complications such as pneumonia or blood clots.

Why is it especially important to maintain or, if necessary, strengthen bones if you have been treated for breast cancer?

- **Premature bone loss.** Among women who have had chemotherapy, bone loss may occur much sooner than it normally might, as observed in a study at Dana-Farber Cancer Institute and Brigham and Women's Hospital that measured changes in bone density among 49 premenopausal women receiving chemotherapy. Over the course of a year, bone density decreased 7 percent at the spine and 4 percent at the hip in 35 women who were pushed into an early menopause. Accelerated bone loss occurred to a lesser extent among those who didn't experience menopause, although this was not considered statistically significant. By contrast, the average rate of bone loss for women after natural menopause is 1 to 2 percent a year and 15 percent over the first ten years. Thus, a woman who undergoes a permanent menopause because of chemotherapy can lose five years' worth of bone mass in a single year.

- **Higher risk of fracture.** A 2005 study using data drawn from the Women's Health Initiative (WHI) compared more than 5,000 women treated for breast cancer to nearly 81,000 women who had no history of breast cancer. With over five years of follow-up, researchers noted that fracture rates in the wrist, spine, and other areas of the body were 15 percent higher among breast cancer survivors than among other women. These higher fracture rates were seen at all sites in the body except the hip. Women diagnosed with breast cancer before age 55 appeared especially vulnerable to spinal fractures. Related research discussed previously suggests that younger survivors are likely to experience a dramatic decline in bone mineral density stemming from menopause brought on by chemotherapy. In premenopausal women, the high proportion of a type of skeletal bone known as trabecular bone is particularly sensitive to an abrupt decrease in estrogen levels. The WHI study, while large and well-designed, needs to be confirmed by further research. The WHI researchers note that if the data hold true in other studies, the number of additional fractures sustained every year may be as high as 13,000 among the two million breast cancer survivors in the United States.

- **Greater risk of spinal fractures.** Breast cancer survivors experience more spinal fractures than women who have not been diagnosed with the condition. In a British study, researchers compared 776 women with no history of breast cancer to 352 women who had just been diagnosed and 82 women who were living with breast cancer that had metastasized to sites in the body other than bone. The 352 women who had been treated for breast cancer had nearly five times the rate of fractures found in women in the general population. Among the 82 who had metastatic disease, the rate of spinal fractures increased twentyfold. Because these fractures were measured by x-ray studies, some were not symptomatic and would otherwise have gone unnoticed.

- **Medication side effects.** A group of anticancer medications called *aromatase inhibitors*, such as exemestane (Aromasin), letrozole (Femara), and anastrozole (Arimidex), are known to speed bone loss and raise the risk of fractures. (One other anticancer medication, tamoxifen, helps preserve bone, particularly at the hip, by acting as an estrogen on the skeleton while blocking its negative effects on the breast.)

- **The long-term outlook.** Improved treatments and earlier detection improve the odds that the majority of women treated for breast cancer will one day die of other causes. Thus, survivors need to focus on undertaking a variety of health measures, such as strengthening bones to help sidestep osteoporosis, that will help them avoid other serious conditions.

The Solutions

Shoring up bones calls for a combination of different approaches, which are discussed here.

- **Bone density testing.** If possible, have a baseline *bone mineral density* (BMD) test before you start cancer treatments. If you are beyond that point, discuss the timing of this baseline test with your physician. A BMD test compares *your* bone mass measurements with *average* bone mass measurements of women in their 30s, which is when peak bone mass is typically achieved. Using that information, the test shows where you fall along a curve that indicates risk for osteoporosis. One BMD test, called *dual energy x-ray absorptiometry* (DXA), uses x-ray beams to calculate bone density, usually at the spine, hip, or wrist, or for the total body. *Ultrasound*, which employs sound waves to measure BMD at the heel, shin, or kneecap, is increasingly being used as well. Its measurements are not as exact as those provided by DXA, but it seems to predict fracture risk. Review the results with your doctor and discuss whether, in addition to weight-bearing exercise and calcium plus vitamin D supplements, you need to consider bone-saving medications, too.

- **Get enough calcium and vitamin D.** Calcium paired with vitamin D (which better enables your body to absorb calcium) is essential for healthy, strong bones. When adding up your daily intake, consider your diet first, then add what you need through supplements.

  Recently, a Women's Health Initiative study published in *New England Journal of Medicine* in 2006 raised questions about whether calcium and vitamin D supplements reduce hip fractures. Over the course of seven years, the study detailed a small, though significant, increase in bone density at the hip, yet no dip in the rate of fractures among those who took supplements compared to those who did not. It's wise to note, though, that many of the participants—more than 36,000 healthy women ages 50 to 79—were taking estrogen replacement therapy and had normal bone density when they joined the study. More than 40 percent failed to take calcium and vitamin D supplements regularly. And, some experts concluded, the 400 IU of vitamin D_3 prescribed in the study may not have been sufficient.

Currently, the daily recommendation for calcium is 1,000 mg for women ages 31 through 50 and 1,200 mg for women 51 and older. Nutrition experts at Dana-Farber Cancer Institute recommend 1,200 mg to 1,500 mg of daily calcium during and after chemotherapy, particularly if early menopause occurs, and while taking aromatase inhibitors such as exemestane (Aromasin), letrozole (Femara), and anastrozole (Arimidex), notes senior clinical nutritionist Stacy Kennedy, M.P.H., RD/LDN. Depending on your age, this may be somewhat higher than normal, although still within safe limits. (Women who have had kidney stones or who have high calcium levels because of breast cancer metastases to the bones should check with their doctors regarding the recommended dose.)

Check the label on the supplements for the amount of calcium in each pill, tablet, or chew (this may be deceptive, so look for the words "elemental calcium," as in "500 mg of elemental calcium"). Calcium citrate is most easily absorbed; calcium carbonate, which costs less, is best taken with meals to aid in absorption. Skip supplements derived from oyster shells, which may have higher lead levels. Coral calcium is questionable, too, because of pollution and environmental concerns. Take calcium supplements in divided doses at different times of day because your body can only absorb about 500 mg to 600 mg of calcium at one time.

Daily intake of vitamin D is currently set at 200 IU between ages 31 and 50; 400 IU between ages 51 and 70; and 600 IU afterward. These recommendations were made by the Institute of Medicine in 1997 and are in the process of evolving, so speak with your doctor about what is best for you. Current evidence suggests a higher vitamin D intake of 800 IU to 1,000 IU is necessary to reduce fractures for the average woman age 50 or older. Sunlight helps activate vitamin D in the skin. In northern regions, lack of sunlight during winter days often prompts vitamin D deficiencies that a higher dose helps address. For women over age seventy who avoid sun exposure as much as possible, Kennedy adds that the recommended intake climbs to 1,000 IU. While these amounts may be higher than normal depending on age, they remain within safe limits.

New research suggests that vitamin D_3 (cholecalciferol) is three times as potent as vitamin D_2 (ergocalciferol). It raises vitamin D blood levels for a longer period of time. Good sources of vitamin D_3 are fatty fishes, juices supplemented with calcium and vitamin D_3, and cod liver oil. Check multivitamin and supplement labels as well as juice labels to see which form of vitamin D you are taking.

Vitamin K, magnesium, phosphorus, and other nutrients play lesser, though still important, roles in strengthening bones. A healthy diet and a daily multivitamin will supply these.

- **Engage in weight-bearing exercise.** Inactivity actually slows bone formation. By contrast, the right weight-bearing exercises help maintain bone density at the three most common fracture sites: the wrists, spine, and hips. Activities that stress bone through impact or by prompting tendons to tug against bone are considered weight-bearing. Walking and strength training are two good examples. Walking only affects bones in the lower body, while regular strength-training sessions can help keep bones throughout the body healthy. Generally, these activities are safe and possible at any age.

- **Fix falling hazards.** Good balance—which can be undermined by aftereffects of breast cancer surgery—is essential to avoid falls that may end in fractures. Performing the balance exercises and stretches in our program will help. Fixing falling hazards in your home, clothes, and footwear as explained in Chapter 10 is very important, too.

- **Consider other factors.** Certain medications, such as glucocorticoids, excessive thyroid hormones, and antiseizure drugs, contribute to bone loss, while the side effects of others, such as dizziness, may cause falls. Some health problems, such as anorexia, liver disease, hyperparathyroidism, disorders that affect mineral absorption, and Parkinson's disease or other neurological disorders, may have an impact on bone density or increase the odds of falling, too. Discuss your medications and health history with your doctor, who can decide what measures, if any, should be taken.

- **Discuss bone-saving medications with your doctor.** If osteoporosis is documented by a BMD test, the American Society of Clinical Oncology 2003 guidelines recommend considering bisphosphonate therapy, such as alendronate (Fosamax), ibandronate (Boniva), or risedronate (Actonel). Other medications may include calcitonin (Miacalcin); parathyroid hormone (Forteo); and possibly raloxifene (Evista). Which are right for you depends on many factors, including your breast cancer status; risks for other medical conditions; current medications; and which sites in your body have significant bone loss. If possible, see a specialist at a skeletal health clinic, such as the Skeletal Health and Osteoporosis Center at Brigham and Women's Hospital in Boston, or see an endocrinologist who specializes in caring for people with osteoporosis and osteopenia.

CHAPTER 3

Combating Lymphedema

After breast cancer surgery that included the removal of many lymph nodes, Kristen Pluntze, a cyclist and runner, felt mightily unsure of how her body might react to exercise. "All I heard was that you don't want to do anything with that arm, you don't want to get lymphedema," she recalls. "So for a few weeks afterward I was scared to even move my arm."

Her anxiety is understandable. When lymph fluid backs up because lymph node surgery or radiation has altered lymph channels, mild to severe swelling occurs. Usually, this is apparent in the arm, which may become quite noticeably enlarged. Less frequently, it occurs in the torso, a condition called *truncal lymphedema* in which swelling or fullness might appear on the breast, at scar lines, over the collarbone, or elsewhere on the chest or back. Lymphedema can be very uncomfortable and may become a chronic problem. Certainly, no woman wants to do anything that might set this cycle in motion.

At one time, doctors routinely advised women who had had lymph nodes removed or radiation to the nodes during the course of breast cancer treatment to avoid heavy lifting and repetitive movements with the affected arm. Sports that required forceful, repeated arm strokes were ruled out, too. Only recently have researchers and breast cancer activists begun to challenge this advice. In fact, rather than triggering lymphedema, some researchers theorize that progressive, properly performed exercises gradually widen remaining lymph channels, thereby improving the flow of lymph.

This chapter explains lymphedema and presents current advice on strategies to reduce the risk for developing it and to ease it. New research now underway on the impact of exercise is described, too. If you had surgery to remove lymph nodes or radiation treatments to the underarm or collarbone area, it is wise to review the information here.

The Lymphatic System

The thin, milky fluid called *lymph* collects in spaces between cells before seeping into the channels that carry it through the body. Lymph contains water, fat, bacteria, infection-fighting cells, and fragments of blood cells. Just as your blood circulates through vessels of various sizes that branch off throughout the body, lymph moves through a similar network of far more thin-walled channels. The largest lymph channels feed back into the bloodstream through two ducts at the base of the neck. Lymph channels, bean-size *lymph nodes*, and other lymphoid tissues and organs, such as the thymus gland and spleen, make up the *lymphatic system*.

Unlike blood, which is actively pumped by your heart, lymph is pushed through this system by various dynamic actions, such as muscle contractions, pressure created by breathing, and motion in organs around lymph channels. Valves within the lymphatic channels keep lymph fluid flowing in one direction. Clusters of lymph nodes positioned in strategic areas, such as the groin, underarm, neck, and knees, filter the lymph (see Figure 3.1). This filtering process enables the body to remove foreign or flawed material and catch intruders like bacteria and viruses so that immune system cells congregating in the lymph nodes can help finish them off.

What Are the Axillary Nodes?

Axilla is the medical term for your underarm, or armpit. This area is home to the axillary nodes, which are the major drainage sites for the lymphatic system in the breast. Axillary nodes are divided

FIGURE 3.1 The Lymphatic System

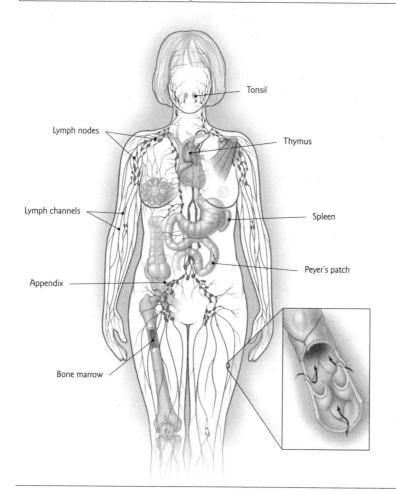

The lymphatic system filters excess fluid and protein that collects in spaces between cells and then returns it to the bloodstream through two ducts in the base of the neck. The system consists of lymph channels that branch throughout the body, clusters of lymph nodes, and certain organs, including the tonsils, adenoids, thymus gland, spleen, and bone marrow. Lymphocytes—blood cells that fight off infection—are manufactured in the bone marrow and the thymus gland. The spleen and lymph nodes serve as filtering stations through which lymph fluid passes. Lymph channels in the breast flow outward through clusters of lymph nodes in the underarm (axilla), upward through clusters of nodes in the collarbone, and inward through clusters of nodes behind the breastbone (also see Figure 3.2). Other sites where lymph nodes congregate include the groin, neck, abdomen, pelvis, and chest. Lymphatic tissue crops up in many organs in the body. In the small intestine, it appears as oval-shaped Peyer's patches.

   This illustration also shows an enlarged section of a lymph channel. Lymph channels, or vessels, may be as large as a vein or as small as very tiny capillaries. The thin-walled channels are composed of overlapping cells, so fluid collecting between body cells seeps into them quite easily. Valves keep lymph fluid flowing in one direction. If surgery or radiation therapy alters lymph channels, the flow of lymph may be slowed or blocked.

into three levels based on their relationship to the pectoralis minor, a muscle that fans across your chest wall from your shoulder to the ribs close to your breastbone (see Figure 3.2).

- Level I nodes can be found in the lower underarm by placing your hand there and pressing the fat pad against your ribs. Often they are difficult to feel, though, because they can blend into the fat pad.
- Level II nodes rest high up in the underarm directly beneath the pectoralis minor.
- Level III nodes are found between the top border of the pectoralis minor and the collarbone. These nodes are hard to feel even on a slender woman with thin chest wall muscles.

Lymph Node Surgery

If invasive breast cancer is suspected, the surgeon usually removes one or more lymph nodes. A specially trained doctor called a *pathologist* examines these nodes under a microscope to see if cancer cells are present. This information helps determine the stage of the cancer. *Positive nodes*—that is, nodes containing cancer cells—indicate cancer has spread regionally beyond the breast. *Negative* nodes mean cancer is less likely to have spread to distant sites, although cancer cells may travel beyond the breast via blood vessels as well as through lymphatic channels.

What Is Axillary Dissection?

Axillary dissection is the removal of one or more levels of underarm lymph nodes. Surgeons once removed all three levels of lymph nodes, but research has shown that if cancerous cells do spread, positive nodes will first be found in the Level I region. It's unusual for cancerous cells to skip Level I and go to Level II. Only rarely will cancerous cells skip Levels I and II, yet be found in Level III. Knowing this—and hoping to leave undisrupted lymphatic channels behind to minimize the chance that lymphedema will occur—surgeons began to take only the 10 to 20 lymph nodes commonly found in the Level I and II regions.

What Is Sentinel Node Biopsy?

As many as two-thirds of the women who undergo traditional lymph node surgery will be happy to learn that there is no evidence of cancer in the nodes. Yet even when Level III lymph nodes are left intact, substantial numbers of these women will develop lymphedema. A newer, less invasive procedure may help many women sidestep this problem. During *sentinel node biopsy*, the surgeon uses a radioactive tracer or blue dye to track the flow of lymph from the affected breast to the first (*sentinel*) node it reaches (see Figure 3.2). The sentinel node is removed, possibly along with one or two other nodes clinging to it. Sometimes more

FIGURE 3.2 Sentinel Node Biopsy

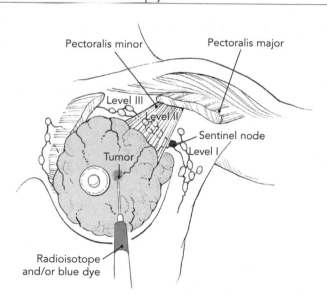

To help determine the stage of an invasive cancer, the axillary (underarm) lymph nodes are examined under the microscope for cancer cells. In traditional lymph node surgery, the surgeon removes Level I and II nodes. Removal of these nodes disrupts lymph channels and may injure nerves. In sentinel node biopsy, the surgeon locates the first node into which the tumor drains (the sentinel node) and examines it for cancer cells. To identify the sentinel node, the surgeon injects the tumor with a radioactive tracer or blue dye, which travels through the breast lymph channels to the first node in the underarm chain. The sentinel node is removed and examined microscopically for signs of cancer.

than one node takes up the tracer or dye. If so, all such nodes are removed. A pathologist examines the sentinel node or nodes, sometimes first during surgery and then always in more detail afterward. If the sentinel node is cancer-free, other nodes downstream from it also are presumed to be negative and are left in place. If the sentinel node contains cancer cells (positive), a traditional axillary dissection is performed to check other nodes.

The Lymphedema Cycle

Any time lymph channels are altered—whether by surgery, radiation, infection, or other causes—fluid backup can occur. As lymph collects, there are fewer available channels for it to pass through, creating a bottleneck. Sometimes this happens only briefly within a few days of breast cancer surgery because lymph channels were cut or otherwise blocked, perhaps by swelling in surrounding tissues. In this case, lymphedema usually is mild and goes away fairly quickly with simple treatments, such as raising the arm or pumping the muscles by squeezing a ball. More commonly, though, lymphedema occurs later on. According to the National Cancer Institute (NCI), it may be noticed within a few months of cancer treatment or many years afterward.

How Often Does Lymphedema Develop?

An estimated one in four women treated for breast cancer will develop arm lymphedema. Certain factors make this more likely. A review of several studies published in the *Journal of the National Cancer Institute* noted that lymphedema occurred in 17 percent of women who also had underarm lymph nodes removed. Among women who also had radiation to this region as well as to the breast, 41 percent developed lymphedema. The greater the number of lymph nodes removed, the higher the risk for lymphedema. Poor nutrition and obesity also played roles, possibly by compromising wound healing.

Other sources suggest as many as 30 percent of women who have traditional lymph node surgery may end up with lymphedema. However, research has been hampered by differing defing of lymphatic channels. For example, wear gloves while washing dishes, using tools, or gardening. Apply insect repellent and sunscreen, as necessary. Try to avoid pet scratches. An electric razor, waxing, or laser hair removal can protect against nicks if you wish to remove underarm hair. If you prefer a razor blade, stand in front of a mirror and take care to avoid nicks. Leave cuticles uncut during a manicure.

- **Attend quickly to cuts, burns, scrapes, and scratches.** Cleanse the area well with antibacterial soap. Apply antibiotic ointment, such as bacitracin or Neosporin, and cover it with a bandage. If you see signs of infection—redness, warmth, or swelling—call your doctor for advice. You may need an antibiotic.
- **Be aware of extremes.** Extreme cold can cause chapping and cracks in the skin, so wrap up warmly in cold weather. Extreme heat can boost lymph production, so limit time spent in the hot sun and avoid hot tubs, steam rooms, saunas, and overly hot water while bathing or washing dishes.
- **Keep lymph channels open.** Tight elastic sleeves, narrow bra straps, heavy shoulder bags, and overly snug bracelets or accessories may put too much pressure on vulnerable remaining lymph channels, possibly causing them to collapse. Avoiding constrictive items like these helps keep lymph channels open.
- **Use compression appropriately.** Compression garments or compression bandages help when applied before swelling starts. Before engaging in vigorous exercise or activities that involve repetitive arm movements, such as lifting weights, running, rowing, or raking, put on a well-fitted compression sleeve or well-fitted compression bandages that you have been taught how to apply (see "Easing Lymphedema" sidebar). Simply buying a sleeve without having the fit checked may cause problems if, for example, the garment fits at the wrist but is too tight or too loose at the upper arm.
- **Be prepared for air travel.** If you have been diagnosed with lymphedema, the National Lymphedema Network (NLN) recommends wearing a compression garment that fits

What Are the Warning Signs of Lymphedema?

If you notice these warning signs, call your doctor for advice and use methods you have been taught to help relieve the problem.

- A heavy, full, or tight sensation in your arm, underarm, or torso (your shirt or bra may feel tighter than usual, too)
- Changes such as swelling, trouble moving or flexing the hand or wrist, unusual tightness in rings, bracelets, or watchband
- A rash or reddened, tender, itchy, or overly warm skin on the arm or chest of the side where you had surgery or radiation, especially if these symptoms also are associated with a fever or if you feel like you have the flu

initions. In some studies, self-reports of any skin tightness might be counted, while other studies might count only women with objectively measured limb or skin changes. So it's hard to say how many women really do develop lymphedema.

Over the years, breast cancer surgery has become more minimal. Similar advances are taking place in lymph node surgery, too. If these changes alter lymph channels less, fewer women may experience lymphedema. Already this is seen with sentinel node biopsy, which requires the removal of far fewer lymph nodes than traditional axillary dissection.

Two large prospective, randomized trials currently compare traditional axillary surgery with sentinel node biopsy. In the United States, a multicenter trial called the National Adjuvant Breast and Bowel Project (NSABP B-32) enrolled more than 5,600 women between May 1999 and February 2004. Participants are still being surveyed for the possibility of developing lymphedema, and these results have yet to be published. In the Axillary Lymphatic Mapping Against Nodal Axillary Clearance (ALMANAC) trial in Europe, more than 1,000 women were randomly assigned to sentinel node biopsy or axillary dissection. At 18 months after surgery, arm swelling affected approximately twice as many of the women who had had axillary dissection compared to those who had sentinel node biopsy: 14 percent versus 7 percent. It's important to note that some of the women who initially had a sentinel node biopsy went on to have axillary dissection. Nonetheless, for the purposes of a clean statistical analysis, they were included in the sentinel node group when the data were analyzed. If these women had been counted as part of the axillary dissection group, the percentage of women experiencing arm swelling in the sentinel node group would drop substantially. Hopefully, as these patients are followed over the years, the true rate of lymphedema in those who had sentinel node biopsy alone without further axillary surgery or radiation will be reported.

Is It Temporary or Permanent?

Temporary (transient) lymphedema goes away within six months without causing significant skin changes. Long-lasting (chronic) lymphedema occurs in cycles that may be hard to halt. A cycle starts when remaining lymph channels cannot keep lymph draining quickly enough. If signs are noticed early, encouraging lymph to drain through raising the arm, gentle exercise, and compression often helps (see "Easing Lymphedema" sidebar).

If early signs are ignored, the pressure of the fluid and accumulating proteins and other potentially damaging substances can lead to permanent changes in the skin. *Fibrosis*, which sometimes is a side effect of radiation, too, stiffens the tissues. Problems then compound quickly: affected tissues have less oxygen to keep them healthy; drainage is compromised by increasing distances between lymph channels pushed apart by swelling; immune cells called *macrophages*, which clear away cellular debris, become less active. Eventually, the risk rises for minor infections and *cellulitis*, a spreading infection in the skin and deeper tissue marked by a warm, tender area and sometimes fever, chills, and blisters.

Reducing the Risk for Lymphedema

Advice on reducing your risk for lymphedema tends to be grounded in an understanding of physiology, rather than data from rigorous studies. Infection, heat, burns, or repetitive, prolonged activity involving the affected arm boost lymph production, which may then overburden remaining lymph channels. Constricting lymph channels slows or blocks the easy flow of lymph. The strategies in this section stem from recommendations made by the National Lymphedema Network and other expert sources. Because every woman's situation is unique, you should discuss these strategies with your surgeon or doctor.

- **Minimize risks, maximize quality of life.** Being thoughtful about decreasing risks makes sense, especially when tips for doing so encourage healthy habits. "It's easier to minimize possible risks for developing lymphedema and the swelling caused by it than it is to get rid of lymphedema once you have it," says Nancy J. Roberge, P.T., D.P.T., M.Ed., a physical therapist who specializes in caring for men and women who have had axillary dissection for breast and other cancers. Being afraid of triggering lymphedema through the least possible slip, however, impairs your quality of life. Ask your surgeon or doctor how high your risk is for lymphedema and discuss which of the tips in this section are most important for you to follow. Personal circumstances differ, but lymphedema is more likely to occur if you:
  - Had 10 or more lymph nodes removed for diagnosis
  - Had extensive surgery
  - Had radiation to the underarm or collarbone areas
  - Are overweight or obese
- **Care for your skin.** Keep skin clean, dry, and supple by applying a hypoallergenic moisturizer on arm and hand daily (do it twice daily during winter months). Soaps that leave your skin feeling dry and tight, such as antibacterial soaps, strip away protective oils, making skin more likely to chap and crack and thus potentially providing entry for bacteria. For daily use, choose gentle soaps with a pH close to neutral, such as Neutrogena, Dove, or Basis. Take steps to avoid injuries and other sources of skin cuts or punctures because infections that may follow might cause scarring and narrow-

snugly from wrist to underarm because decreased air pressure during the flight causes lymph to move more slowly through the lymphatic system and pool in the spaces surrounding cells. Compression garments offer support that mimics air pressure at sea level, so that lymph fluid more readily seeps into lymph channels. "Any time I fly, I put on a garment," says Diane, who had 39 lymph nodes removed more than a decade ago and had experienced some swelling in her arm and wrist. "That seems to help." Stay hydrated and move around every half hour or hour, which also helps keep lymph from pooling.

What if you have *not* been diagnosed with lymphedema but did have lymph nodes removed or had radiation? Discuss your risks for lymphedema with your surgeon or doctor and decide whether wearing a compression sleeve or bandages during air travel is a sensible precaution.

- **Alert health care providers.** Consider wearing a lymphedema alert bracelet (available at lymphnet.org or 800-541-3259). At health care visits, ask to have blood pressure, blood tests, shots, acupuncture, and IVs reserved for the arm unaffected by lymph node surgery or radiation, if possible. Avoid heat packs on the affected side. If you had lymph node surgery or radiation on both sides, it may be possible to take blood pressure and perhaps give injections or place IVs in your leg.
- **Care for yourself.** Help support your immune system by eating well, exercising, keeping your weight in a healthy range (or losing weight if necessary), getting sufficient rest, and engaging in relaxation. This is especially important now because the lymphatic network in certain regions may be weakened, allowing infection in these areas to get a better foothold. A healthy weight has the added benefit of reducing your risk for developing lymphedema.

Where Does Exercise Fit In?

Exercise has pluses and minuses where lymphedema is concerned. Muscle action and deep breathing help move lymph along, but vigorous exercise speeds blood flow and perhaps lymph production. Erring on the side of caution, doctors have often warned breast cancer survivors away from exercise, especially activities that require forceful, repetitive arm movements.

New thinking suggests that a gradual, progressive strength-training program may actually minimize the chance of developing lymphedema by helping dilate, or widen, remaining lymphatic channels in the underarm and around the shoulder. Widened channels would be better able to handle increases in the flow of lymph prompted by more vigorous exercise or a problem like an arm infection. Stretches can ease tightness and scarring that block lymph flow. Walking and other activities that enhance cardiovascular fitness boost general health, and the deep breathing prompted by such exercise helps lymph flow. Swimming, in fact, offers these benefits while the water applies supportive compression. If you are at risk for lymphedema or have had it, talk to your doctor or a lymphedema therapist about how to exercise safely and follow the precautions in Chapter 9. Modifications of our program that take the extent of your condition into account may be necessary.

Researchers continue to delve into the effects of arm movements and arm exercises on lymphedema. One such study has been mounted by Dana–Farber Cancer Institute and Row as One Institute (rowasone.org), an organization founded by Olympic gold medal–winning rower Holly Metcalf to empower women physically and mentally. The researchers will look at experienced and novice rowers who are breast cancer survivors and experienced and novice rowers who have not had breast cancer. Hopefully, this study will help us learn more about whether rowing—a sport with cardiovascular benefits that builds strength—might have positive or negative effects on the development of lymphedema in breast cancer survivors.

Easing Lymphedema

If you do notice signs of lymphedema, rest with the affected arm raised on a pillow, which allows gravity to assist lymph in draining back into the central circulation. Call your doctor for advice. Deep-breathing exercises, which help relieve lymphedema of the arm, also may be of some help for women with truncal lymphedema—that is, lymphedema of the breast, chest area, or back. A reservoir for lymph called the *cysterna chyli* is situated behind your navel. "When you breathe deeply, your diaphragm moves up and down, creating pressure changes in the abdomen and chest that help pump lymph fluid," explains Bonnie Lasinski, P.T., CLT-LANA. Some women may need *complete decongestive therapy* (CDT), a combination of specialized massage known as *manual lymphatic drainage*, compressive bandaging, proper skin care and diet, specific exercises, and compression garments. This therapy should be performed by a professional trained in these techniques, who will be able to teach self-care steps as well.

Karen Jackson, the founder and CEO of Sisters Network, Inc., a national African American breast cancer survivorship organization, suffered a serious bout of lymphedema after having a lumpectomy followed by radiation and chemotherapy. "My hand would swell, and at times the fluid reached my elbow and I experienced a burning sensation and numbness. It was difficult to hold the telephone or carry a handbag." She sought help from a lymphedema therapist, but found visits quite costly. "Insurance and personal funding will not indulge you in that," she says wryly. "I paid attention and learned how to do it for myself." Her daily self-care steps work reliably to help keep fluid from building up. Jackson, who was 50 when she received her diagnosis and is now 62, leads an active life. She walks, swims, bicycles, lifts light weights, and has been known to canoe. "I've been able to overcome lymphedema and, I must say, not by following all of the lymphedema instructions, but by trial and error and seeing what works for me."

Because no national standards for lymphedema therapists exist, the National Lymphedema Network recommends finding a professional who:

- Is licensed in a related health field, such as a registered nurse, physical therapist, or occupational therapist
- Has completed 135 hours of CDT coursework, two-thirds of which should be devoted to practical lab work
- Has completed college-level courses in human anatomy, physiology, and/or pathology

(continued)

Easing Lymphedema, *continued*

Your cancer care team may be able to refer you to someone. The NLN website lists referrals to treatment centers and trained professionals. The Lymphology Association of North America website lets you search by state for certified lymphedema therapists (CLTs) who have passed the organization's qualifying exam (see Resources). Word of mouth also may help you find a therapist with expertise in working with women who have had breast cancer, notes Anne Hooley-Buckley, P.T.

What Are the Warning Signs of Lymphedema?

If you notice these warning signs, call your doctor for advice and use methods you have been taught to help relieve the problem.

- A heavy, full, or tight sensation in your arm, underarm, or torso (your shirt or bra may feel tighter than usual, too)
- Changes such as swelling, trouble moving or flexing the hand or wrist, unusual tightness in rings, bracelets, or watchband

- A rash or reddened, tender, itchy, or overly warm skin on the arm or chest of the side where you had surgery or radiation, especially if these symptoms also are associated with a fever or if you feel like you have the flu

initions. In some studies, self-reports of any skin tightness might be counted, while other studies might count only women with objectively measured limb or skin changes. So it's hard to say how many women really do develop lymphedema.

Over the years, breast cancer surgery has become more minimal. Similar advances are taking place in lymph node surgery, too. If these changes alter lymph channels less, fewer women may experience lymphedema. Already this is seen with sentinel node biopsy, which requires the removal of far fewer lymph nodes than traditional axillary dissection.

Two large prospective, randomized trials currently compare traditional axillary surgery with sentinel node biopsy. In the United States, a multicenter trial called the National Adjuvant Breast and Bowel Project (NSABP B-32) enrolled more than 5,600 women between May 1999 and February 2004. Participants are still being surveyed for the possibility of developing lymphedema, and these results have yet to be published. In the Axillary Lymphatic Mapping Against Nodal Axillary Clearance (ALMANAC) trial in Europe, more than 1,000 women were randomly assigned to sentinel node biopsy or axillary dissection. At 18 months after surgery, arm swelling affected approximately twice as many of the women who had had axillary dissection compared to those who had sentinel node biopsy: 14 percent versus 7 percent. It's important to note that some of the women who initially had a sentinel node biopsy went on to have axillary dissection. Nonetheless, for the purposes of a clean statistical analysis, they were included in the sentinel node group when the data were analyzed. If these women had been counted as part of the axillary dissection group, the percentage of women experiencing arm swelling in the sentinel node group would drop substantially. Hopefully, as these patients are followed over the years, the true rate of lymphedema in those who had sentinel node biopsy alone without further axillary surgery or radiation will be reported.

Is It Temporary or Permanent?

Temporary (transient) lymphedema goes away within six months without causing significant skin changes. Long-lasting (chronic) lymphedema occurs in cycles that may be hard to halt. A cycle starts when remaining lymph channels cannot keep lymph draining quickly enough. If signs are noticed early, encouraging lymph to drain through raising the arm, gentle exercise, and compression often helps (see "Easing Lymphedema" sidebar).

If early signs are ignored, the pressure of the fluid and accumulating proteins and other potentially damaging substances can lead to permanent changes in the skin. *Fibrosis*, which sometimes is a side effect of radiation, too, stiffens the tissues. Problems then compound quickly: affected tissues have less oxygen to keep them healthy; drainage is compromised by increasing distances between lymph channels pushed apart by swelling; immune cells called *macrophages*, which clear away cellular debris, become less active. Eventually, the risk rises for minor infections and *cellulitis*, a spreading infection in the skin and deeper tissue marked by a warm, tender area and sometimes fever, chills, and blisters.

Reducing the Risk for Lymphedema

Advice on reducing your risk for lymphedema tends to be grounded in an understanding of physiology, rather than data from rigorous studies. Infection, heat, burns, or repetitive, prolonged activity involving the affected arm boost lymph production, which may then overburden remaining lymph channels. Constricting lymph channels slows or blocks the easy flow of lymph. The strategies in this section stem from recommendations made by the National Lymphedema Network and other expert sources. Because every woman's situation is unique, you should discuss these strategies with your surgeon or doctor.

- **Minimize risks, maximize quality of life.** Being thoughtful about decreasing risks makes sense, especially when tips for doing so encourage healthy habits. "It's easier to minimize possible risks for developing lymphedema and the swelling caused by it than it is to get rid of lymphedema once you have it," says Nancy J. Roberge, P.T., D.P.T., M.Ed., a physical therapist who specializes in caring for men and women who have had axillary dissection for breast and other cancers. Being afraid of triggering lymphedema through the least possible slip, however, impairs your quality of life. Ask your surgeon or doctor how high your risk is for lymphedema and discuss which of the tips in this section are most important for you to follow. Personal circumstances differ, but lymphedema is more likely to occur if you:
  - Had 10 or more lymph nodes removed for diagnosis
  - Had extensive surgery
  - Had radiation to the underarm or collarbone areas
  - Are overweight or obese
- **Care for your skin.** Keep skin clean, dry, and supple by applying a hypoallergenic moisturizer on arm and hand daily (do it twice daily during winter months). Soaps that leave your skin feeling dry and tight, such as antibacterial soaps, strip away protective oils, making skin more likely to chap and crack and thus potentially providing entry for bacteria. For daily use, choose gentle soaps with a pH close to neutral, such as Neutrogena, Dove, or Basis. Take steps to avoid injuries and other sources of skin cuts or punctures because infections that may follow might cause scarring and narrow-

ing of lymphatic channels. For example, wear gloves while washing dishes, using tools, or gardening. Apply insect repellent and sunscreen, as necessary. Try to avoid pet scratches. An electric razor, waxing, or laser hair removal can protect against nicks if you wish to remove underarm hair. If you prefer a razor blade, stand in front of a mirror and take care to avoid nicks. Leave cuticles uncut during a manicure.

- **Attend quickly to cuts, burns, scrapes, and scratches.** Cleanse the area well with antibacterial soap. Apply antibiotic ointment, such as bacitracin or Neosporin, and cover it with a bandage. If you see signs of infection—redness, warmth, or swelling—call your doctor for advice. You may need an antibiotic.

- **Be aware of extremes.** Extreme cold can cause chapping and cracks in the skin, so wrap up warmly in cold weather. Extreme heat can boost lymph production, so limit time spent in the hot sun and avoid hot tubs, steam rooms, saunas, and overly hot water while bathing or washing dishes.

- **Keep lymph channels open.** Tight elastic sleeves, narrow bra straps, heavy shoulder bags, and overly snug bracelets or accessories may put too much pressure on vulnerable remaining lymph channels, possibly causing them to collapse. Avoiding constrictive items like these helps keep lymph channels open.

- **Use compression appropriately.** Compression garments or compression bandages help when applied before swelling starts. Before engaging in vigorous exercise or activities that involve repetitive arm movements, such as lifting weights, running, rowing, or raking, put on a well-fitted compression sleeve or well-fitted compression bandages that you have been taught how to apply (see "Easing Lymphedema" sidebar). Simply buying a sleeve without having the fit checked may cause problems if, for example, the garment fits at the wrist but is too tight or too loose at the upper arm.

- **Be prepared for air travel.** If you have been diagnosed with lymphedema, the National Lymphedema Network (NLN) recommends wearing a compression garment that fits snugly from wrist to underarm because decreased air pressure during the flight causes lymph to move more slowly through the lymphatic system and pool in the spaces surrounding cells. Compression garments offer support that mimics air pressure at sea level, so that lymph fluid more readily seeps into lymph channels. "Any time I fly, I put on a garment," says Diane, who had 39 lymph nodes removed more than a decade ago and had experienced some swelling in her arm and wrist. "That seems to help." Stay hydrated and move around every half hour or hour, which also helps keep lymph from pooling.

What if you have *not* been diagnosed with lymphedema but did have lymph nodes removed or had radiation? Discuss your risks for lymphedema with your surgeon or doctor and decide whether wearing a compression sleeve or bandages during air travel is a sensible precaution.

- **Alert health care providers.** Consider wearing a lymphedema alert bracelet (available at lymphnet.org or 800–541–3259). At health care visits, ask to have blood pressure, blood tests, shots, acupuncture, and IVs reserved for the arm unaffected by lymph node surgery or radiation, if possible. Avoid heat packs on the affected side. If you had lymph node surgery or radiation on both sides, it may be possible to take blood pressure and perhaps give injections or place IVs in your leg.

- **Care for yourself.** Help support your immune system by eating well, exercising, keeping your weight in a healthy range (or losing weight if necessary), getting sufficient rest, and engaging in relaxation. This is especially important now because the lymphatic network in certain regions may be weakened, allowing infection in these areas to get a better foothold. A healthy weight has the added benefit of reducing your risk for developing lymphedema.

Where Does Exercise Fit In?

Exercise has pluses and minuses where lymphedema is concerned. Muscle action and deep breathing help move lymph along, but vigorous exercise speeds blood flow and perhaps lymph production. Erring on the side of caution, doctors have often warned breast cancer survivors away from exercise, especially activities that require forceful, repetitive arm movements.

New thinking suggests that a gradual, progressive strength-training program may actually minimize the chance of developing lymphedema by helping dilate, or widen, remaining lymphatic channels in the underarm and around the shoulder. Widened channels would be better able to handle increases in the flow of lymph prompted by more vigorous exercise or a problem like an arm infection. Stretches can ease tightness and scarring that block lymph flow. Walking and other activities that enhance cardiovascular fitness boost general health, and the deep breathing prompted by such exercise helps lymph flow. Swimming, in fact, offers these benefits while the water applies supportive compression. If you are at risk for lymphedema or have had it, talk to your doctor or a lymphedema therapist about how to exercise safely and follow the precautions in Chapter 9. Modifications of our program that take the extent of your condition into account may be necessary.

Researchers continue to delve into the effects of arm movements and arm exercises on lymphedema. One such study has been mounted by Dana-Farber Cancer Institute and Row as One Institute (rowasone.org), an organization founded by Olympic gold medal–winning rower Holly Metcalf to empower women physically and mentally. The researchers will look at experienced and novice rowers who are breast cancer survivors and experienced and novice rowers who have not had breast cancer. Hopefully, this study will help us learn more about whether rowing—a sport with cardiovascular benefits that builds strength—might have positive or negative effects on the development of lymphedema in breast cancer survivors.

Easing Lymphedema

If you do notice signs of lymphedema, rest with the affected arm raised on a pillow, which allows gravity to assist lymph in draining back into the central circulation. Call your doctor for advice. Deep-breathing exercises, which help relieve lymphedema of the arm, also may be of some help for women with truncal lymphedema—that is, lymphedema of the breast, chest area, or back. A reservoir for lymph called the *cysterna chyli* is situated behind your navel. "When you breathe deeply, your diaphragm moves up and down, creating pressure changes in the abdomen and chest that help pump lymph fluid," explains Bonnie Lasinski, P.T., CLT-LANA. Some women may need *complete decongestive therapy* (CDT), a combination of specialized massage known as *manual lymphatic drainage*, compressive bandaging, proper skin care and diet, specific exercises, and compression garments. This therapy should be performed by a professional trained in these techniques, who will be able to teach self-care steps as well.

Karen Jackson, the founder and CEO of Sisters Network, Inc., a national African American breast cancer survivorship organization, suffered a serious bout of lymphedema after having a lumpectomy followed by radiation and chemotherapy. "My hand would swell, and at times the fluid reached my elbow and I experienced a burning sensation and numb-ness. It was difficult to hold the telephone or carry a handbag." She sought help from a lymphedema therapist, but found visits quite costly. "Insurance and personal funding will not indulge you in that," she says wryly. "I paid attention and learned how to do it for myself." Her daily self-care steps work reliably to help keep fluid from building up. Jackson, who was 50 when she received her diagnosis and is now 62, leads an active life. She walks, swims, bicycles, lifts light weights, and has been known to canoe. "I've been able to overcome lymphedema and, I must say, not by following all of the lymphedema instructions, but by trial and error and seeing what works for me."

Because no national standards for lymphedema therapists exist, the National Lymphedema Network recommends finding a professional who:

- Is licensed in a related health field, such as a registered nurse, physical therapist, or occupational therapist
- Has completed 135 hours of CDT coursework, two-thirds of which should be devoted to practical lab work
- Has completed college-level courses in human anatomy, physiology, and/or pathology

(continued)

Easing Lymphedema, *continued*

Your cancer care team may be able to refer you to someone. The NLN website lists referrals to treatment centers and trained professionals. The Lymphology Association of North America website lets you search by state for certified lymphedema therapists (CLTs) who have passed the organization's qualifying exam (see Resources). Word of mouth also may help you find a therapist with expertise in working with women who have had breast cancer, notes Anne Hooley-Buckley, P.T.

CHAPTER 4

After Lumpectomy

Shortly after Dara* learned she had breast cancer, she had the breast-saving surgery known as lumpectomy. Afterward, the site where surgery had been performed was very sensitive and tight. "I slowly worked my way through that a little bit at a time," she says. Radiation therapy, a treatment that is coupled with lumpectomy, was the next step. Several weeks into her radiation treatments, Dara joined a rowing team in Boston through We Can Row, an offshoot of the Row as One Institute founded by Olympic rower Holly Metcalf that was specifically designed for women who have been treated for breast cancer. By that point, Dara's stiffness and discomfort had improved. To build up to rowing as a team, the group engaged in stretches and light exercises under the guidance of an experienced physical therapist before working on oar skills for short periods of time. These activities presented no problem. "It was great," Dara says. "This was so energizing after a few months of just lying around and not doing anything much."

How might a lumpectomy affect you? During your recovery and sometimes later on as well, it may interfere with mundane tasks or hold you back from activities you enjoy. It is likely to raise fewer

---

* Not her actual name

of the physical concerns typical after more extensive breast surgery, although the experience varies from woman to woman. Another rower who also had a lumpectomy noted, for example, that muscle stiffness and tightness because of changes wrought by radiation curtailed her ability to move her arm and shoulder freely for the better part of two years. This chapter describes lumpectomy and notes the most common challenges that may crop up. In Chapters 9 through 12 you'll find safety tips and workouts designed to improve your overall health and address issues that do arise.

The Surgery

Breast cancer surgery and the therapies that follow it are lifesaving. Yet these treatments may create their own set of challenges. Here, we explain your anatomy before surgery and changes after lumpectomy.

Anatomy Before Surgery

Between the soft outer skin of the breast and the underlying pectoral (chest) muscles covering the ribs lies a landscape of fat interwoven with milk-producing glandular tissue. The milk glands are shaped like stalks of broccoli. The fluffy ends of the stalks, which are called lobules, produce the milk. The stalks themselves are the *ducts* that carry milk from the lobule to the nipple during breast-feeding (see Figure 4.1).

Intricate networks carve pathways between the glands and through the fatty portions of the breast. Nerves richly endow the breast skin, nipples, and areola with sensation. Arteries, veins, and smaller blood vessels deliver oxygen and nutrients to the tissues and cart off waste products. Lymphatic channels carry thin, milky fluid called lymph to small bean-shaped organs called lymph nodes that appear in clusters near the outer breast in the axilla (underarm), around the collarbone, and in the chest. The nodes, which are part of the immune system, filter out germs and foreign matter and produce infection-fighting white blood cells. Blood vessels and lymphatic channels are laced through the fatty tissue

FIGURE 4.1 Breast Anatomy

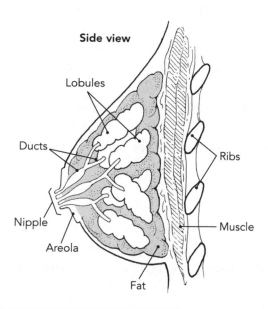

Side view

Lobules

Ducts

Ribs

Nipple

Muscle

Areola

Fat

Composed primarily of fat and glandular tissue, the breast also has nerves, arteries, veins, and lymphatic channels that carry lymph fluid to the lymph nodes. The lobules are milk-producing glands, and the ducts carry the milk from the lobules to the nipple during breast-feeding. Breast cancer usually starts inside the gland. In time, it may break through the gland wall and spread through the lymph channels or blood vessels to other parts of the body.

surrounding ducts and lobules. There are no blood vessels or lymphatic channels within the ducts and lobules themselves.

Anatomy After Lumpectomy

The breast-saving surgery best known as *lumpectomy* also may be called *wide local excision*, *partial mastectomy*, *quadrantectomy*, or *tylectomy*. During a lumpectomy, the surgeon removes cancerous tissue plus a slender rim of surrounding healthy tissue known as a *clean margin* or *negative margin*. After excising the tissue, the surgeon inks it with six different colors (one for each side) so it will be possible to tell which edge corresponds with a given edge within the surgical cavity. That way, a second—or even third—surgery called a *reexcision* can be performed if necessary after a pathologist examines the tissue, or *specimen*. Reexcision of selected additional tissue is done if cancer cells are found near one or more of the edges of the specimen (*positive margin*). This technique minimizes the amount of tissue removed while helping to optimize safe, clean margins. When less tissue is removed, the breast is more likely to look much as it did originally. As more tissue is removed, a smaller breast and change in shape become more likely. The nipple and areola are left intact during a lumpectomy. The underlying pectoral muscles also are untouched (see Figure 4.2).

The Challenges

Certain activities and tasks may become more difficult, though not necessarily impossible, after a lumpectomy and radiation therapy, the form of breast cancer treatment with which this surgical

FIGURE 4.2 Lumpectomy

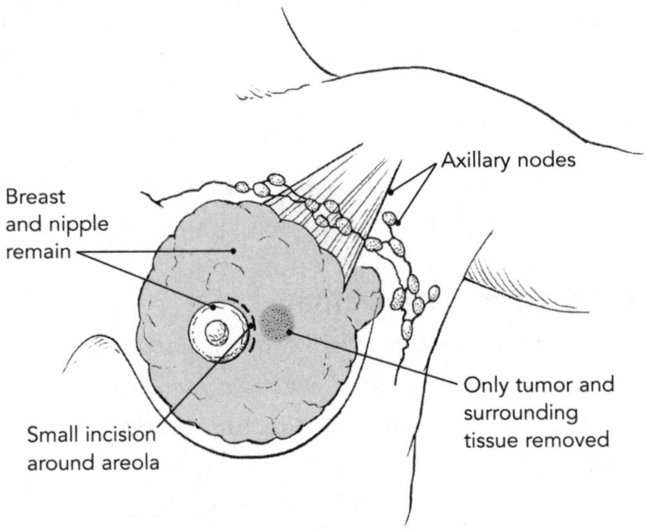

During a lumpectomy, the surgeon removes only the cancerous tissue and a margin of normal surrounding tissue. The nipple and areola are left intact. For cancers in a central part of the breast, the surgeon may place the incision at the border of the areola to obtain the best cosmetic effect and allow a woman to wear a bathing suit or low-cut dress without a scar showing. If the tumor is invasive, lymph nodes under the arm may be removed for analysis (see Chapter 3 for more information).

procedure is coupled. Surgery and radiation may affect posture, flexibility, strength, and energy in the following ways.

How Is Posture Affected?

Pain and tightness after surgery can make good posture—particularly keeping your shoulders back and down away from your ears—difficult to achieve, at least for a while. You may adopt *protective posturing*—head tilted forward, shoulder raised and hunched, elbow bent so that your hand rests across your belly, and body bending forward at the waist—as a result. The discomfort stems from pain and tightness in the area where the incision was closed.

Lingering aftereffects that sometimes occur with radiation therapy might have an impact on posture, too. Just as you may notice skin changes for many months after radiation therapy—for example, a reddened or darkened area that usually lightens over time—subtle changes also continue beneath the surface. Radiation may stiffen and shorten the pectoral muscles, for example, one effect of a condition known as *fibrosis* that can prompt thickened skin tissue, too. Because these changes can go on for up to two years or so after radiation therapy, continuing to perform the recommended stretches regularly rather than stopping once you achieve a full range of motion will be very helpful.

How Is Flexibility Affected?

You may notice no changes whatsoever in flexibility—that is, the range of motion through which you can comfortably move a joint like your shoulder. Or you might find that discomfort from your surgery or, later on, stiffness in chest muscles from radiation makes it difficult to raise your arm at the shoulder. Pain stemming from surgery, skin tension, scarring, or costochondritis from radiation (see sidebar "Costochondritis") all can contribute to temporary or permanent motion restriction. Keep in mind that even a temporary way to dodge discomfort may become permanent unless you begin to gently expand these limits. One example is a *frozen shoulder*, which stems from severely limiting your range of motion in

Massage Therapy

Postsurgical pain plus noticeable tightness where breast tissue was removed during a lumpectomy and the incision was closed may affect posture and shoulder flexibility. So, too, might changes in tissue beneath the skin, such as stiffness in the chest muscles that may occur over time after radiation therapy. Sometimes such tightness and stiffness makes it hard to breathe deeply and move comfortably. These sensations may be noticeable during the initial recovery period or persist beyond it.

Scar tissue at the surgical site may pucker and pull uncomfortably. Sometimes *cording*, a phenomenon in which muscle tendons or larger lymphatic channels stick to the undersurface of the skin, occurs in the underarm as scar tissue forms where lymph nodes were removed. When a woman lifts her arm, the skin in the underarm area pulls these structures outward and a vertical cord can be seen.

Massage therapy by a trained physical therapist or massage therapist may be needed to ease tightness, release cording and scar tissue, and help regain shoulder mobility. Your surgeon can evaluate you to see if this would help you heal. Information on finding an experienced physical therapist or massage therapist appears in Chapter 1.

your shoulder and arm for a prolonged time after surgery. Tightness in the joint results and worsens until normal movements become acutely painful.

Stretching exercises—if necessary, coupled with massage therapy (see sidebar "Massage Therapy") or physical therapy that may include heat, massage, passive stretches, and specific exercises— will help you regain a comfortable range of motion. It's wise to continue doing stretches regularly because skin and deep tissue changes due to radiation may affect flexibility for many months after treatment is finished.

How Are Muscles and Activities Affected?

No muscles were directly affected by your surgery. Thus, once you've recovered from surgery, you may find all of your usual activities easy to do. Possibly, although by no means always, radiation therapy may cause temporary discomfort in skin and stiff-

Costochondritis

Radiation beams typically skim the top surface of the ribs underlying the breast, touching upon cartilage that connects the breastbone to each rib and the fascia, a thin covering that encases the ribs like a piece of plastic wrap and is richly endowed with nerves. Sometimes this causes *costochondritis*, inflammation and pain in the fascia, ribs, and cartilage that may wax and wane. It's most noticeable when you firmly touch this area or during a cough or sneeze.

ness in chest muscles and surrounding tissues. If you do experience these side effects, routine tasks—reaching up to take a package off a high shelf, lifting groceries or heavy objects—may become uncomfortable or difficult to do. Normally, the pectoral muscles help you flex and rotate your arms at the shoulders, bring your arms in toward your body, and push or press against resistance. Examples of activities that might be temporarily affected are:

- Turning the steering wheel while driving
- Pulling open heavy doors, especially sliding glass doors
- Pushing revolving doors
- Push-ups
- Cross-country skiing
- Tennis
- Golf
- Rowing
- Swimming (overhead strokes, such as the crawl)

How Is Energy Affected?

Fatigue is a potent side effect of surgery. It follows on the heels of radiation and chemotherapy, too. As your body heals, it channels energy toward repairing and rebuilding cells. It's common for fatigue to last four to six weeks after radiation treatment, according to the National Cancer Institute (NCI). Dips in red blood cells stemming from certain chemotherapy drugs may make fatigue vary from week to week. Many women find their exhaustion snowballs as treatment proceeds. Other medical and emotional issues also may play a role. Discuss persistent exhaustion with your doctor, who can help identify root problems and suggest solutions. Some small, preliminary studies suggest light to moderate walking or other activities help boost energy in those coping with cancer.

How Can I Help My Body Recover?

To recover as fully as possible, you need to regain comfortable upright posture and establish balance in flexibility and strength on both sides. Building energy and endurance is essential, too. Each element of our program will help you move forward at a gradual pace. Walking and posture checks are essential when you are recovering from your surgery. Stretching and balance exercises are key, too. Strength exercises will help you regain lost ground or stake out new ground. Chapters 9 through 12 contain information on when to begin exercising and how to exercise safely, as well as the actual workouts.

Recovery from a lumpectomy usually occurs fairly quickly. Often, you can begin returning to most activities within one to two weeks. However, radiation therapy is likely to slow you down again, so it will be longer before you truly feel like yourself.

When Can I Begin Exercising?

Obtain your surgeon's permission before you start our exercise program or add new exercises. Review the exercises you plan to do and discuss possible limitations, such as not reaching above shoulder height during the early healing phase. If you had a lumpectomy, you are unlikely to have many limitations, but it is wise to check. This is especially important if you also had lymph node surgery.

Make sure you understand the tips for exercising safely explained in Chapter 9. You'll find exercises, workouts, and a plan for getting started in Chapters 10 through 12. The right timing for beginning to exercise varies depending on the speed of your recovery and the advice of your surgeon.

Typically, you'll be encouraged to start walking on the day you have your lumpectomy. Usually, any activities that you feel comfortable doing are safe at this point, too. The first week after surgery, you may be able to add the balance and stretching exercises. Once you can easily stand upright and have regained a full or comfortable range of motion, you should be able to begin our light strength-training exercises. Generally, this workout can be added to your program two weeks after surgery. If you had lymph nodes removed, follow the timing for sentinel node surgery or axillary dissection instead (see Table 10.1, "The Right Timing," in Chapter 10). If you had axillary dissection, your surgical drains should be removed before you begin doing stretching and strength-training exercises.

CHAPTER 5

After Mastectomy

At 62, Liz Usborne takes great pleasure in playing a good game of tennis several times a week. A swim instructor for many years, she also enjoys time spent in the pool doing the breaststroke, side-stroke, and crawl. Yet just four years ago, after a lumpectomy followed by months of chemotherapy and then, unexpectedly, a mastectomy because a second cancer had initially gone unnoticed, Liz wasn't doing much of anything. "It took me 10 minutes to get up off the floor," she says. Quite sick at that time after chemotherapy and her second surgery, she spent hour upon hour in bed. The immobility, she believes, contributed to a frozen shoulder—not on the side where her surgery had been done, but on the opposite side where she lay resting for so long. Fortunately, months of extensive physical therapy and her own determination set her back on the road to recovery. "I'm 180 degrees better," says Liz. "Now everything is pretty much back to normal."

Karen, 47, had a far easier time after her mastectomy a year ago. She didn't need to have chemotherapy or radiation therapy, and her recovery was smooth and fairly swift. After her incision healed, her flexibility was unimpaired. She can lift her arm in a sweeping arc to illustrate this. "I do notice that my right arm is no longer as strong as my left," she says. "I baby it now. For months, I didn't lift heavy things with it because I worried about lymphedema."

How might a mastectomy affect you? During your recovery and sometimes later on as well, it may interfere with mundane tasks or hold you back from activities you enjoy. Concerns vary from woman to woman, depending partly on the extent of your mastectomy. This chapter describes different surgeries and details the most common physical challenges that may crop up. In Chapters 9 through 12 you'll find safety tips and workouts designed to improve your overall health and address issues that do arise.

The Surgery

Breast cancer surgery is lifesaving. Yet it does create its own set of challenges. Here, we explain your anatomy before surgery and changes after a mastectomy when a woman does not choose to have reconstructive surgery.

Anatomy Before Surgery

Between the soft outer skin of the breast and the underlying pectoral (chest) muscles covering the ribs lies a landscape of fat interwoven with milk-producing glandular tissue. The milk glands are shaped like stalks of broccoli. The fluffy ends of the stalks, which are called lobules, produce the milk. The stalks themselves are the ducts that carry milk from the lobule to the nipple during breastfeeding (see Figure 5.1).

Intricate networks carve pathways between the glands and through the fatty portions of the breast. Nerves richly endow the breast skin, nipples, and areola with sensation. Arteries, veins, and smaller blood vessels deliver oxygen and nutrients to the tissues and cart off waste products. Lymphatic channels carry thin, milky fluid called lymph to small bean-shaped organs called lymph nodes that appear in clusters near the outer breast in the axilla (underarm), around the collarbone, and in the chest. The nodes, which are part of the immune system, filter out germs and foreign matter and produce infection-fighting white blood cells. Blood vessels and lymphatic channels are laced through the fatty tissue surrounding ducts and lobules. There are no blood vessels or lymphatic channels within the ducts and lobules themselves.

FIGURE 5.1 Breast Anatomy

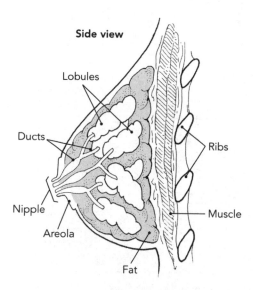

Composed primarily of fat and glandular tissue, the breast also has nerves, arteries, veins, and lymphatic channels that carry lymph fluid to the lymph nodes. The lobules are milk-producing glands, and the ducts carry the milk from the lobules to the nipple during breast-feeding. Breast cancer usually starts inside the gland. In time, it may break through the gland wall and spread through the lymph channels or blood vessels to other parts of the body.

Anatomy After Mastectomy

During a mastectomy, the entire breast, nipple, and areola (dark circle of skin around the nipple) are removed. There are several variations of mastectomy, which affect different degrees of surrounding lymph nodes and muscles.

- A *simple (total) mastectomy* removes the entire breast, nipple, and areola, but not the lymph nodes or the muscles underneath.
- A *modified radical mastectomy* removes the entire breast, nipple, areola, and pocket of fat containing underarm lymph nodes (axillary nodes) (see Figure 5.2). See Chapter 3 for more information on lymph node surgery.

FIGURE 5.2 Modified Radical Mastectomy

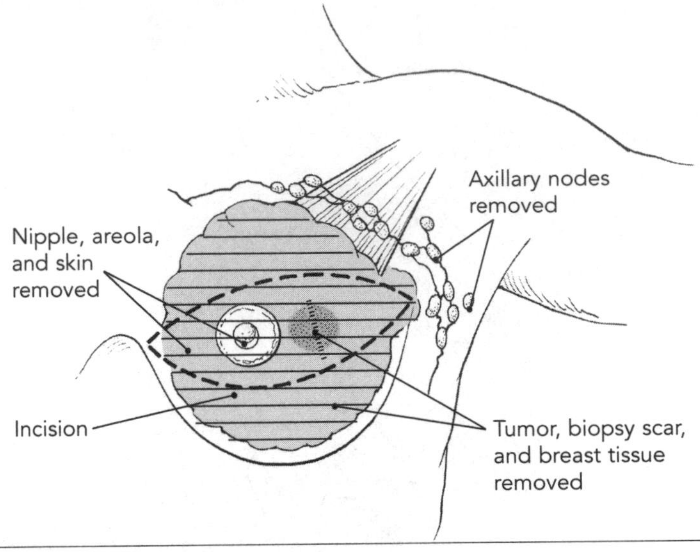

During a modified radical mastectomy, the surgeon makes an incision and removes the breast tissue plus the nipple and areola as well as axillary lymph nodes. If no breast reconstruction is planned, the surgeon removes much of the skin of the breast, also.

- A *radical mastectomy*, which is rarely performed today, removes the entire breast, the pectoral muscles beneath it, and all the underarm lymph nodes up to the collarbone. See Chapter 3 for more information on lymph node surgery.

If you planned to have immediate breast reconstruction, your surgeon performed a *skin-sparing mastectomy*. During this procedure, the surgeon removes the nipple, aerola, and recent incisions from breast cancer biopsies while sparing as much of the native skin of the breast as possible. The skin serves as an envelope to cover the reconstruction. This is particularly helpful when lat flap reconstruction is chosen because it allows the surgeon to take less skin from the back. This may make the reshaped breast look more pleasing cosmetically, too.

If you did not plan to have surgery to reconstruct the breast at the same time as your mastectomy, your surgeon removed sufficient breast skin to achieve a smooth, flat surface on the healed chest wall. This is a *non-skin-sparing mastectomy*. It allows a woman to more comfortably wear a breast form, if she chooses to do so.

The Challenges

Certain activities and tasks may become more difficult, though not necessarily impossible, after a mastectomy. The surgery may affect posture, flexibility, strength, and energy in the following ways.

How Is Posture Affected?

Pain and tightness after surgery can make good posture—particularly keeping your shoulders back and down away from your ears—difficult to achieve, at least for a while. Discomfort often prompts *protective posturing*—head tilted forward, shoulder raised and hunched, elbow bent so that your hand rests across your belly, and body bending forward at the waist. Stretches help ease the discomfort, which stems from skin tightness in the area where the incision was closed and the process of healing.

How Is Flexibility Affected?

Flexibility—that is, the range of motion through which you can comfortably move a joint like your shoulder—is affected in several ways. Raising your arm at the shoulder initially may be quite hard. Pain, skin tension, and scarring all can contribute to temporary or permanent motion restriction. Yet even a temporary way to dodge discomfort may become permanent unless you begin to gently expand these limits. One example is a *frozen shoulder*, which stems from severely limiting your range of motion in your shoulder and arm for a prolonged time after surgery. Tightness in the joint results and worsens until normal movements become acutely painful.

Stretching exercises—if necessary, coupled with massage therapy (see sidebar "Massage Therapy") or physical therapy that may include heat, massage, passive stretches, and specific exercises—will help you regain a comfortable range of motion. If you had

Massage Therapy

Noticeable tightness on the chest where breast tissue was removed during a mastectomy and the incision was closed may affect posture and shoulder flexibility. Sometimes such tightness makes it hard to breathe deeply and comfortably. These sensations are common during the initial recovery period and may persist beyond it.

Scar tissue at the surgical sites may pucker and pull uncomfortably. Sometimes *cording*, a phenomenon in which muscle tendons or larger lymphatic channels stick to the under-surface of skin, occurs in the underarm as scar tissue forms where lymph nodes were removed or at surgical incision sites. When a woman lifts her arm, the skin in the underarm area pulls the muscle outward and a vertical cord can be seen.

Massage therapy by a trained physical therapist or massage therapist may be needed to ease tightness, release cording and scar tissue, and help regain shoulder mobility. Your surgeon can evaluate you to see if this would help you heal. Information on finding an experienced physical therapist or massage therapist appears in Chapter 1.

radiation therapy, it's particularly important to continue doing stretches regularly because skin and deep tissue changes due to radiation may affect flexibility for many months after treatment is finished.

How Are Muscles and Activities Affected?

No muscles were directly affected by your surgery unless you had a radical mastectomy (see next paragraph). Nonetheless, a mastectomy can impinge on shoulder strength and mobility. Temporary or permanent weakness or discomfort makes routine tasks—buttoning a shirt, washing or brushing your hair, reaching up to take a package off a high shelf—difficult. Other examples of activities that might be affected, at least temporarily, are:

- Lifting groceries or heavy objects
- Turning the steering wheel while driving
- Cross-country skiing

- Tennis
- Golf
- Swimming (overhead strokes, such as the crawl)

If you did have a radical mastectomy, the pectoral muscles that lie against the chest wall were removed. Normally, the pectoral muscles help you flex and rotate your arms at the shoulders, bring your arms in toward your body, and push or press against resistance. Thus, strength and mobility are likely to be more seriously compromised. Examples of additional activities that might be affected are:

- Pulling open heavy doors, especially sliding glass doors
- Pushing revolving doors
- Push-ups

How Is Energy Affected?

Fatigue is a potent side effect of surgery. It follows on the heels of radiation and chemotherapy, too. As your body heals, it channels energy toward repairing and rebuilding cells. It's common for fatigue to last four to six weeks after radiation treatment, according to the National Cancer Institute (NCI). Dips in red blood cells stemming from certain chemotherapy drugs may make fatigue vary from week to week. Many women find their exhaustion snowballs as treatment proceeds. Other medical and emotional issues also may play a role. Discuss persistent exhaustion with your doctor, who can help identify root problems and suggest solutions. Some small, preliminary studies suggest light to moderate walking or other activities help boost energy in those coping with cancer.

How Can I Help My Body Recover?

To recover as fully as possible, you need to regain comfortable upright posture and establish balance in flexibility and strength on both sides. Rebuilding energy and endurance is essential, too. Each element of our program will help you move forward at a gradual pace. Walking and posture checks are essential when you are recovering from your surgery. Stretching and balance exercises are key, too. Strength exercises will help you regain lost ground. Chapters 9 through 12 contain information on when to begin exercising and how to exercise safely as well as the actual workouts.

Recovery from a mastectomy may take a while, especially if you also are undergoing chemotherapy. Usually it takes three to six weeks before strength and energy improve enough for you to begin returning to most activities, though it may be longer before you truly feel like yourself.

When Can I Begin Exercising?

Obtain your surgeon's permission before you start our exercise program or add new exercises. Review the exercises you plan to do and discuss any limitations, such as not reaching above shoulder height in the first weeks after surgery during the early healing phase.

Make sure you understand the tips for exercising safely explained in Chapter 9, too. You'll find exercises, workouts, and a plan for getting started in Chapters 10 through 12. The right timing for beginning to exercise varies depending on the speed of your recovery and the advice of your surgeon.

Typically, you'll be encouraged to start walking the day after your surgery. Usually, activities that do not require you to lift your arm higher than shoulder height are safe at this point, too. Within one or two weeks, you may be able to perform the balance exercises also. Two weeks after surgery, as long as your surgical drains have been removed, you may be able to add the stretching exercises. Once you can easily stand upright and have regained a full or comfortable range of motion, you should be able to begin our light strength-training exercises. Generally, this workout can be added four weeks after your surgery.

CHAPTER 6

After Breast Implant Surgery

Two years after having a mastectomy, Ainia* returned to the hospital for reconstructive surgery with a saline implant. The following year, she decided that it would be wise to have a prophylactic mastectomy on her other breast along with surgery to place an implant on that side, too. After each procedure, she found it took time and a lot of exercises before she could move her arm and shoulder comfortably. "I'm a nurse," says Ainia, who was 48 when diagnosed with breast cancer. "So I know the importance of getting your range of motion back. It was painful, very painful, to do my exercises, but I did them." Now 53, she continues to work in a physically demanding job. Just as important, despite some complications following her reconstruction, she enjoys playing basketball and riding a bike with her son.

How might breast implant surgery affect you? During your recovery and sometimes later on as well, it may interfere with mundane tasks or hold you back from activities you enjoy. Concerns vary from woman to woman, depending partly on whether

---

Not her actual name

the procedure was performed at the time of mastectomy or some-time down the road and whether one or both breasts were re-created. This chapter describes breast implant surgery after mastectomy and outlines common physical challenges that may crop up. In Chapters 9 through 12, you'll find safety tips and workouts designed to improve your overall health and address issues that do arise.

The Surgery

Reconstructive surgery is a life-enhancing choice for many women. Yet it does create its own set of challenges. Here, we explain your anatomy before surgery and changes after breast implant surgery.

Anatomy Before Surgery

After a mastectomy removes breast tissue, two closely aligned muscles called the *pectoralis major* and *pectoralis minor* lie directly beneath the skin on the chest wall (see Figures 6.1 and 6.2). Positioned over the ribs, the larger pectoralis major is on top overlapping the smaller pectoralis minor underneath it. The pectoralis major is a thick muscle that originates on the humerus bone of the upper arm and fans out to attach to the collarbone, the breastbone, cartilage at the second through the sixth ribs, and the upper abdominal muscles. The pectoralis minor, a slim, triangular muscle, attaches to the third, fourth, and fifth ribs as well as to the undersurface of the wing bone (scapula) on your back.

Your pectoral muscles have several tasks. The pectoralis major helps you flex and rotate your arm at the shoulder joint and pull it in toward your body. The pectoralis minor helps keep the wing bone flat on your back. The muscles work in concert to help you push or press against resistance, such as when opening a heavy door. Normally the muscles lie flat on the chest wall. During the course of the surgeries performed for implant reconstruction and during tissue expansions, the pectoralis major is actively pushed away from the ribs. The procedures may weaken these muscles, undermine posture, and restrict shoulder motion.

FIGURE 6.1 Chest Muscles: Pectoralis Major

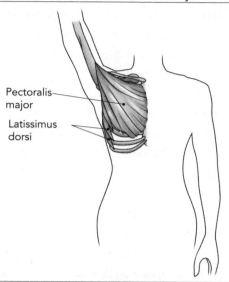

Pectoralis
major

Latissimus
dorsi

The pectoralis major is a thick, fan-shaped muscle on the chest wall. It helps you flex and rotate your arm at the shoulder joint and pull it toward your body. Part of the latissimus dorsi, a broad back muscle, is shown here, too.

FIGURE 6.2 Chest Muscles: Pectoralis Minor

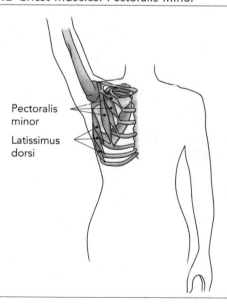

Pectoralis
minor

Latissimus
dorsi

The pectoralis minor is a slim, triangular muscle that lies beneath the pectoralis major. The pectoralis minor helps keep the wing bone (scapula) flat on your back. Part of the latissimus dorsi, a broad back muscle, is shown here, too.

Anatomy After Implant Surgery

If you had small breasts, your surgeon may have been able to place a small permanent breast implant beneath the pectoralis major muscle during a single procedure. Generally, though, implant surgery is a two-step process. During the first surgery, a tissue expander will be placed.

After the mastectomy is completed, the pectoralis major and pectoralis minor muscles are exposed. After separating the muscles along the length of their fibers, the surgeon gently lifts the pectoralis major away from the ribs. This forms a pocket into which the expander is placed (see Figure 6.3). A small quantity of saline (salt water) may be injected through a needle into the valve, or port, of the expander. Sometimes just placing the expander puts sufficient stress on the skin and muscles, so the surgeon will choose not to inflate the expander with saline right away. A drain

FIGURE 6.3 Tissue Expander to Prepare for Implant

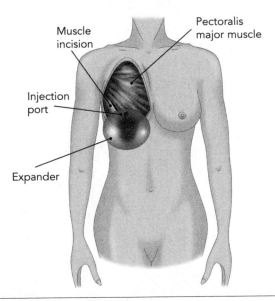

Before a permanent implant is placed, a tissue expander is temporarily inserted under the skin and pectoralis major to gently stretch them, creating a pocket for the implant.

is placed beneath the skin to siphon off excess lymphatic fluid. The surgeon then stitches closed the muscle and then the skin.

After several weeks of healing, the expansion phase begins. Saline is injected through the port into the expander. This will be done every few weeks over the course of several months to gradually and gently stretch the chest wall muscles and overlying skin until the expander is a bit larger than the desired size of the implant. Overfilling this way helps to stretch the skin and muscle enough to create a more natural fold of skin below the breast. When the expansion is completed, the surgeon makes a small incision to remove the expander and place the permanent implant. Like the expander, the implant will be positioned in a pocket between the pectoralis major and pectoralis minor (see Figure 6.4).

Each time the expander was inflated, pushing the pectoral muscles away from the chest wall, Rosalita experienced painful muscle spasms that lasted for days. "Tasks as simple as opening a jar lid, pushing a revolving door, or even turning the steering wheel of my car hard to one side were temporarily impossible,"

FIGURE 6.4 Side View of Implant

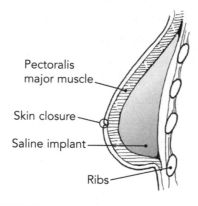

A view from the side. The breast tissue has been removed during a mastectomy. The skin lies directly over the pectoralis major. The implant is placed in a pocket formed between the smaller and larger pectoral muscles.

she recalls. "My shoulder—and even my arm and hand—weakened considerably." Only as the pain and muscle spasms eased would the weakness begin to subside, but repeated tissue expansions chipped away at her strength and flexibility. Physical therapy and a light weight regimen helped restore both.

Sometimes the plastic surgeon chooses to cut the median pectoral nerve. This nerve, which reaches to the outer portions of the pectoral muscles, passes along signals that enable the muscles to contract and helps maintain the outer contour of the chest. The added laxity of the muscle after the nerve is cut may enhance the appearance of the reconstructed breast in some women. However, the chest muscles affected will be slightly weaker than the muscles on the other side of the body.

The Challenges

Certain activities and tasks temporarily may become more difficult, though not necessarily impossible, after surgeries to place a tissue expander and implant. This may be noticeable after each tissue expansion, too. Posture, flexibility, arm and shoulder strength, and energy may be affected in the following ways.

How Is Posture Affected?

Good posture depends on the counterbalancing forces of the pectoral muscles pulling the shoulder forward while back muscles pull it backward. The pectoralis minor is tasked with helping to keep the wing bone (scapula) flat on your back. Weakness in the chest muscles may cause the shoulder to hunch forward and makes standing up straight difficult.

Protective posturing—head tilted forward, shoulder raised and hunched, elbow bent so that your hand rests across your belly, and body bending forward at the waist—can occur because of discomfort after surgery. The discomfort stems from tightness in the area where the incision was closed after surgery and from the tissue expander pressing against pectoral muscles, which may set off muscle spasms. Some of this pain eases as the muscle spasms relax a few days after the tissue expander is placed or after each injec-

Massage Therapy

Pressure on the pectoral muscles or even muscle spasms from the tissue expander or breast implant, and tightness on the chest where skin is snugly sewn together, can affect posture and shoulder flexibility. Both pectoral muscles are used to lying flat on the chest. Once an expander is placed, the larger pectoralis major muscle is pushed away from its usual position. Each time saline is added to the expander, the muscle may go into a painful spasm much like a charley horse. These sensations may occur after surgery and after each expansion. Sometimes they may occur intermittently beyond the recovery period.

Scar tissue at the surgical sites may pucker and pull uncomfortably. Sometimes *cording*, a phenomenon in which muscle tendons or larger lymphatic channels stick to the under-surface of skin, occurs in the underarm as scar tissue forms where lymph nodes were removed or at surgical incision sites. In the case of implant surgery, cording can appear at the outer edge of the pectoral muscles. When a woman lifts her arm, the skin pulls the edge of the pectoral muscle outward.

Massage therapy by a trained physical therapist or massage therapist may be needed to ease tightness, release cording and scar tissue, and help regain shoulder mobility. Your plastic surgeon can evaluate you to see if this would help you heal. Information on finding an experienced physical therapist or massage therapist appears in Chapter 1.

tion of saline. At that point, the remaining discomfort is due to skin tightness and the process of healing.

How Is Flexibility Affected?

Initially, raising your arm at the shoulder will be nearly impossible. Spasms, pain, or scarring in the muscles in this area—the pectorals (chest), coracobrachialis (rear of the shoulder through the underarm and down the upper arm), and latissimus dorsi (back)—can all contribute to temporary or permanent motion restriction. Keep in mind that voluntarily limiting your range of motion as a temporary way to dodge discomfort may become permanent unless you begin to gently expand these limits. One example is a frozen shoulder, which stems from severely limiting your range of motion in your shoulder and arm for a prolonged time after surgery. Tightness in the joint results and worsens until normal movements become acutely painful.

Stretching exercises—if necessary, coupled with massage therapy (see sidebar "Massage Therapy") or physical therapy that may include heat, massage, passive stretches, and specific exercises—will help you regain a comfortable range of motion. If you had radiation therapy, it's particularly important to continue doing stretches regularly because skin and deep tissue changes due to radiation may affect flexibility for many months after treatment is finished.

How Are Muscles and Activities Affected?

Normally, the pectoral muscles help you flex and rotate your arms at the shoulders, bring your arms in toward your body, and push or press against resistance. Sometimes temporary or permanent weakening of the pectoral muscles affects arm strength to the point where mundane tasks—twisting open a tight lid on a jar or pulling open a heavy drawer of pots in the kitchen—become difficult or uncomfortable to do. Some other examples of activities that might be affected are:

- Washing or brushing your hair
- Pulling open heavy doors, especially sliding glass doors
- Pushing revolving doors
- Turning the steering wheel while driving
- Push-ups
- Cross-country skiing
- Tennis
- Golf
- Swimming (overhead strokes, such as the crawl)

Usually, these changes are temporary and resolve as healing occurs and muscle strength and flexibility returns.

How Is Energy Affected?

Fatigue is a potent side effect of surgery. It follows on the heels of radiation and chemotherapy, too. As your body heals, it channels energy toward repairing and rebuilding cells. It's common for fatigue to last four to six weeks after radiation treatment, according to the National Cancer Institute (NCI). Dips in red blood cells stemming from certain chemotherapy drugs may make fatigue vary from week to week. Many women find their exhaustion snowballs as treatment proceeds. Other medical and emotional issues also may play a role. Discuss persistent exhaustion with your doctor, who can help identify root problems and suggest solutions. Some small, preliminary studies suggest light to moderate walking or other activities helps boost energy in those coping with cancer.

How Can I Help My Body Recover?

To recover as fully as possible, you need to regain comfortable, upright posture, establish balance in flexibility and strength on both sides of your body, and strengthen chest and shoulder muscles. Rebuilding energy and endurance is essential, too. Each element of our program will help you move forward at a gradual pace. Walking, posture checks, and stretching are essential when you are recovering from the surgeries. Balance and strength exercises will help you regain lost ground. Chapters 9 through 12 contain information on when to begin exercising and how to exercise safely, as well as the actual workouts.

Usually it takes at least several weeks to recover from surgery to place an expander and, later, an implant. Because the tissue expansions occur over several months and the implant requires a second surgery, recovery happens more than once and may seem very drawn out. Between surgeries, and particularly after the tissue expansions are completed, your strength and energy should rebound enough for you to return to most activities.

When Can I Begin Exercising?

Obtain your surgeon's permission before you start our exercise program or add new exercises. Review the exercises you plan to do and discuss any limitations, such as not reaching above shoulder height in the first weeks after surgery during the early healing phase.

Make sure you understand the tips for exercising safely explained in Chapter 9, too. You'll find exercises, workouts, and a plan for getting started in Chapters 10 through 12. The right timing for beginning to exercise varies depending on the speed of your recovery and the advice of your surgeon.

Typically, you'll be encouraged to start walking the day after your surgery. Usually, activities that do not require you to lift your arm higher than shoulder height are safe at this point, too. Within 1 or 2 weeks, you may be able to perform the balance exercises also and then go on to add the stretching exercises 3 to 6 weeks after surgery. Once you can easily stand upright and have regained a full or comfortable range of motion, you should be able to begin our light strength-training exercises. Generally, this workout can be added about 12 weeks after your surgery.

CHAPTER 7

After TRAM Flap Surgery

Ten months after her surgeon rotated the two strong muscles running down her central abdomen up to her chest during a TRAM flap reconstruction following a double mastectomy, Michele Forsten and her life partner, Barbara, traveled to an all-women's week at Club Med for a much-needed vacation. The sun beat down brightly, the water beckoned, and Michele, then an active 47-year-old, decided to learn how to water-ski. Rising up on water skis for the first time is hard for anyone. For Michele, it proved nearly impossible. "Getting pulled out of the water was excruciatingly painful. Also, my center of gravity seemed to be different, and I wasn't sure how to compensate for that." she recalls. "On the same trip I tried playing volleyball for the first time after my surgery. It was pretty painful—it was hard to extend myself and hit the ball."

Even now, three years after having reconstructive surgery, Michele finds that her balance is still thrown off. Last February, she fell while scrambling to catch a piece of paper that was flying off down a New York street. "I wondered if it was because I didn't have the strength in my abdominal muscles, which normally might have stopped me from falling forward," she says. Sitting up from a lying-down position, which was once a cinch, is now a trial. And a pulling sensation across her chest makes her feel like she is wearing a Cross-Your-Heart bra all the time.

At the opposite end of the spectrum is Joan Lawhon's recollection of the weeks following her TRAM flap surgery. Postsurgery pain was eye-opening, and initially she found it impossible to straighten up. "The surgery on the upper part of my body was not the issue for me," she says. "It was the *lower* part of my body that was more painful." Yet her recovery moved ahead so quickly that she remembers dancing salsa and merengue just weeks after her surgery. Six years later, only a cramping sensation in the area from which the muscle was moved bothers her at times.

How might having TRAM flap surgery affect you? During your recovery and sometimes later on as well, it may interfere with mundane tasks or hold you back from activities you enjoy. Concerns vary widely from woman to woman. Some of the differences may reflect how lax or tight your tummy was before surgery and whether one or both of the central abdominal muscles known medically as the rectus abdominis were used during reconstruction. These muscles belong to a larger group of core muscles that support and stabilize the spine. Weakness in this sturdy foundation may pave the path toward back problems. This chapter describes TRAM flap surgery and outlines common physical challenges that may crop up. In Chapters 9 through 12, you'll find safety tips and workouts designed to improve your overall health and address issues that do arise.

The Surgery

Reconstructive surgery is a life-enhancing choice for many women. Yet it does create its own set of challenges. Here, we explain your anatomy before surgery and changes after TRAM flap reconstruction.

Anatomy Before Surgery

Every muscle in your body is anchored to at least two bones. The rectus abdominis muscles, perhaps more popularly known as the "six-pack abs" of infomercials, are two elongated, rectangular muscles that form the central panel of your abdomen. Each one extends the full length of the abdominal wall, reaching from the

FIGURE 7.1 Abdominal Muscles: Rectus Abdominis

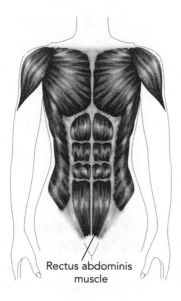

Rectus abdominis
muscle

The rectus abdominis muscles consist of two vertical muscles that make up the center of the abdominal wall. They run from below the chest wall to the pubic bone.

front-central fifth, sixth, and seventh ribs down to the pubic bone (Figure 7.1).

When one breast is being reconstructed, one of the muscles is used. When both breasts are being reconstructed, both muscles may be used, one for each side of the chest. For some women, however, this could weaken the abdomen too much, in which case another type of reconstruction, such as bilateral implants, might be recommended.

Encasing each rectus muscle is the *fascia*, a sheet of thin tissue similar to plastic wrap. On the underside of the muscle, the fascia separates the rectus muscle from the abdominal organs. The blood supply for the muscle runs along its undersurface. In the upper portion of the muscle, the blood vessel is called the *superior epigastric artery*. In the lower portion of the muscle, the blood vessel is called the *deep inferior epigastric artery*. One or both of these vessels will be used to secure a good blood supply for the TRAM flap reconstruction.

Your rectus muscles help you maintain good posture and bend forward. These strong core body muscles play roles in strength, posture, balance, and flexibility. You use them during many tasks and activities, such as lifting, bending, cycling, and swimming.

Anatomy After TRAM Flap Surgery

During TRAM flap surgery, the *r*ectus *a*bdominis *m*uscle and a portion of abdominal skin and fat—that is, the TRAM flap—are rotated from the lower abdomen to the chest wall. The *T* in TRAM comes from the *t*ransverse (horizontal) incision made by the surgeon at the beginning of this procedure (see Figure 7.2). Shaped like an eye, this elliptical incision extends from hip bone to hip bone and includes the underlying fat. One rectus muscle is exposed, and the fascia surrounding it on either side is cut open.

FIGURE 7.2 TRAM Flap

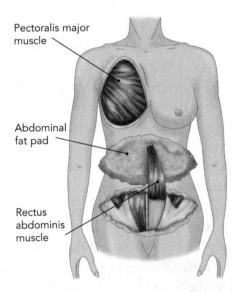

In TRAM flap surgery, skin, fat, and muscle from the lower abdomen are transferred to the chest to reconstruct the breast.

Then the surgeon detaches the muscle from the spot where it is anchored to the pubic bone and cuts the blood supply to the lower part of the muscle, too. Now the muscle flap with its attached fat and skin is ready to use to reconstruct the breast.

In a *pedicle flap* procedure, the blood supply to the upper portion of the muscle is maintained and the flap is flipped from its position in the abdomen to the chest (Figure 7.3). The surgeon creates a tunnel with skin and fat on top and muscle below that reaches from the abdomen to the chest. At the point where the muscle flap attaches to the ribs, it is rotated and passed through the tunnel. The superior epigastric artery, which was left untouched, will serve as the blood supply for the flap. Because nerves were disrupted when the tunnel was created for the pedicle to pass through, the abdominal wall may become permanently numb.

FIGURE 7.3 Pedicle TRAM Flap

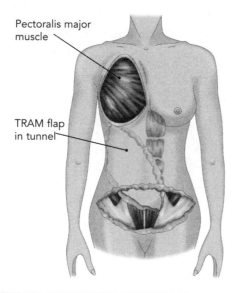

Pectoralis major muscle

TRAM flap in tunnel

In pedicle TRAM flap surgery, the muscle flap is only partially detached. It is then tunneled beneath the skin to the chest, where the muscle, skin, and fat from the abdomen are shaped to form the breast mound.

The surgeon next trims, shapes, and sews the flap into place to recreate the breast mound. The skin of the new breast is sewn closed. Afterward, the surgeon turns to the abdomen and sews together the edges of the fascia. A piece of mesh may be positioned over the fascia and sewn into place to further secure the abdominal wall.

A new spot for the umbilicus, or belly button, is fashioned. The surgeon makes a small incision in the wall of the upper abdomen, brings out the umbilicus at this spot, and sews it into place. Finally, the incision on the abdomen is sewn closed. Drains to siphon off the excess lymphatic fluid that accumulates after surgery are placed under the skin of the reconstructed breast and in the abdomen.

A variation of this procedure is a *free* TRAM flap. Instead of leaving part of the muscle and blood supply anchored at the ribs, the surgeon cuts the muscle and blood vessels at both the upper and lower portions of the rectus muscle. The entire flap is then moved from the abdomen to the chest wall (Figure 7.4). Using highly specialized microsurgical techniques, the surgeon forges entirely new connections for the blood vessels. No tunnel is needed to bring transplanted tissue to the chest wall, so this technique creates less disruption to skin and nerves on the front of the abdomen and lower rib cage. As with a pedicle TRAM flap, drains to siphon off the excess lymphatic fluid that accumulates after surgery are placed under the skin of the reconstructed breast and in the abdomen.

The Challenges

Certain activities and tasks may become more difficult, though not necessarily impossible, after TRAM flap surgery. Posture, flexibility, strength, and energy may be affected as follows.

How Is Posture Affected?

The body *core* includes the muscles of the abdomen and back that run between the ribs and pelvis. Strong core muscles minimize

FIGURE 7.4 Free Tram Flap

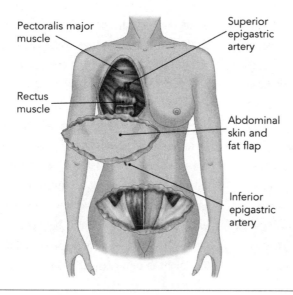

Pectoralis major
muscle

Superior
epigastric
artery

Rectus
muscle

Abdominal
skin and
fat flap

Inferior
epigastric
artery

In free TRAM flap surgery, the rectus muscle plus abdominal fat and skin are completely detached. The blood vessels of the flap are reconnected to blood vessels in the underarm or chest. The flap is then surgically shaped to form the breast mound.

the chance of lower back strain and disk problems. By removing one or two of the many muscles that help build core strength, TRAM surgery weakens the foundation supporting and stabilizing your spine.

For weeks after TRAM surgery, tightness and pain at the abdominal incision can make straightening up completely impossible. Yet consistently bending forward to gain relief eventually shortens the muscles that link your trunk to your legs, such as the hip flexors. *Protective posturing*—head tilted forward, shoulder raised and hunched, elbow bent so that your hand rests across your belly, and body bending forward at the waist—can occur because of discomfort after surgery. Tightness on your chest, where the rectus muscle may be pulling in its new location, and at your abdominal incision, where skin, fat, and muscle were removed, plays into this, too.

Massage Therapy

Noticeable tightness from the pull of the muscle in its new location if a pedicle flap was performed and from the abdominal incision where skin is snugly sewn together can affect posture significantly. Likewise, skin tightness and pain affect flexibility in the shoulder and can make it impossible to comfortably stand up straight with good posture for weeks. This is common during the initial recovery period and may persist beyond it.

Scar tissue at the surgical sites may pucker and pull uncomfortably. Sometimes *cording*, a phenomenon in which muscle tendons or larger lymphatic channels stick to the undersurface of skin, occurs as scar tissue forms where underarm lymph nodes were removed or at surgical incision sites. When a woman lifts her arm, the skin in the underarm area pulls the muscle outward and a vertical cord can be seen.

Massage therapy by a trained physical therapist or massage therapist may be needed to ease tightness, release cording and scar tissue, and help you regain upright posture and flexibility. Your plastic surgeon can evaluate you to see if this would help you heal. Information on finding an experienced physical therapist or massage therapist appears in Chapter 1.

How Is Flexibility Affected?

At first, it may be hard to stand up straight, walk without bending over, or reach overhead. Tightness in your abdomen and hip flexors contributes to these challenges. Shoulder range of motion on the side where you had surgery is likely to be limited, too. After the surgical sites heal, scar tissue sometimes interferes with free range of movement.

Pain and discomfort from surgery can cause you to voluntarily limit your range of motion in your trunk and shoulder. Yet what starts as a temporary way to dodge discomfort may become permanent unless you begin to gently expand these limits. One example is a frozen shoulder, which stems from severely limiting your range of motion in your shoulder and arm for a prolonged time after surgery. Tightness in the joint results and worsens until normal movements become acutely painful.

Stretching exercises—if necessary, coupled with massage therapy (see sidebar, "Massage Therapy") or physical therapy that may include heat, massage, passive stretches, and specific exercises—will help you regain a comfortable range of motion. If you had radiation therapy, it's particularly important to continue stretching regularly because skin and deep tissue changes due to radiation may affect flexibility for many months after treatment is finished.

How Are Muscles and Activities Affected?

Normally, the rectus muscles play key roles in stabilizing the spine and transferring the force of an action from your legs to your core or your core to your arms. When one or both rectus muscles are moved from their usual position in the central abdomen, other muscles must pick up the slack. The transversus abdominis—a broad, deep muscle that encircles your abdomen and back like a girdle—helps here. Strong rectus muscles also keep you from developing a hernia, or weak spot, in the abdominal wall. For this reason, while you are healing, your surgeon will tell you to avoid lifting anything heavy or performing activities that strenuously work this area, such as vigorous sports (walking is fine) and sexual activity, usually for up to six weeks.

The rectus muscles belong to a larger set of core muscles that allow your body to engage in movements essential to daily tasks and active sports such as sitting, standing, walking, bending, lifting, twisting, and reaching. Some examples of athletic activities that might be affected are:

- Sit-ups
- Golf
- Cycling
- Rowing
- Waterskiing
- Windsurfing

How Is Energy Affected?

Fatigue is a potent side effect of surgery. It follows on the heels of radiation and chemotherapy, too. As your body heals, it channels energy toward repairing and rebuilding cells. It's common for fatigue to last four to six weeks after radiation treatment, according to the National Cancer Institute (NCI). Dips in red blood cells stemming from certain chemotherapy drugs may make fatigue vary from week to week. Many women find their exhaustion snowballs as treatment proceeds. Other medical and emotional issues also may play a role. Discuss persistent exhaustion with your doctor, who can help identify root problems and suggest solutions. Some small, preliminary studies suggest light to moderate walking or other activities helps boost energy in those coping with cancer.

How Can I Help My Body Recover?

To recover as fully as possible, you need to regain comfortable upright posture, establish balance in flexibility and strength on both sides, and recruit muscles that can compensate for the loss of the rectus muscle. Rebuilding energy and endurance is essential, too. Each element of our program will help you move forward at a gradual pace. Stretching and posture checks are very important after TRAM flap surgery. Walking—even though at first you may not believe you can possibly put one foot in front of the other—is key, as well. Balance and strength exercises will help you regain lost ground. Chapters 9 through 12 contain information on when to begin exercising and how to exercise safely, as well as the actual workouts.

Recovery from TRAM flap surgery is lengthy, especially if you also are undergoing chemotherapy. Usually it takes six weeks to three months before strength and energy improve enough for you to begin returning to most activities. It may take up to a year before you truly begin to feel like yourself again.

When Can I Begin Exercising?

Obtain your surgeon's permission before you start our exercise program or add new exercises. Review the exercises you plan to do and discuss any limitations, such as not reaching above shoulder height during the early healing phase or not lifting anything heavy for at least six weeks.

Make sure you understand the tips for exercising safely explained in Chapter 9, too. You'll find exercises, workouts, and a plan for getting started in Chapters 10 through 12. The right timing for beginning to exercise varies depending on the speed of your recovery and the advice of your surgeon.

Typically, you'll be encouraged to start walking the day after your surgery. Usually, activities that do not require you to lift your arm higher than shoulder height are safe at this point, too. Within two to four weeks, your surgeon may permit you to start the balance exercises, and between weeks three to six you may be able to add the stretching exercises, too. Once you can easily stand upright and have regained a full or comfortable range of motion, you should be able to begin our light strength-training exercises. Generally, this workout can be added around week 12.

CHAPTER 8

After Latissimus Dorsi
Flap Surgery

At 39, Brooke Donahue is an avid cyclist. Six years ago, she underwent a bone marrow transplant as part of her treatment for breast cancer that had metastasized. During the long weeks of recovery, the walls of her room were plastered with photos of bikes. "I thought, 'My bike, I've got to get back on my bike,'" she recalls. She set an ambitious goal to recover in time to train for and ride in the Pan-Mass Challenge (PMC), a 190-mile bike ride that raises money for research at Dana-Farber Cancer Institute in Boston. Brooke met that goal, then went on to surpass it by riding in her second and third Pan-Mass Challenge and taking a 300-mile tour in Alaska. In 2004, she married one of her fellow PMC bikers. For their honeymoon, they rode the PMC on a tandem bike, Brooke with a bridal veil floating above her cycling gear, her husband sporting a top hat.

To accomplish all of this, Brooke rose to meet numerous challenges. After having a double mastectomy, she chose to have latissimus dorsi (lat) flap surgery. During this procedure, both of the large, sail-shaped lat muscles that fan out across the lower half of the back were rotated to her chest to recreate her breasts.

A cyclist depends on her lat muscles to help propel her up hills as she pulls up on the handlebars and bears down hard on the pedals. After lat flap surgery, Brooke no longer had these strong back muscles, so climbing hills became more difficult. By training under the guidance of Josie Gardiner, she was able to build up muscles that surround and support the lats so that her legs would bear less of the brunt of hill climbs.

If you're not a cyclist like Brooke, how might lat flap surgery affect you? During your recovery and sometimes later on as well, it may interfere with mundane tasks or hold you back from activities you enjoy. Concerns vary from woman to woman, depending partly on whether one or both lat muscles were used. This chapter describes the surgery and details the most common physical challenges that may crop up. In Chapters 9 through 12, you'll find safety tips and workouts designed to improve your overall health and address issues that do arise.

The Surgery

Reconstructive surgery is a life-enhancing choice for many women. Yet it does create its own set of challenges. Here, we explain your anatomy before surgery and changes after lat flap reconstruction.

Anatomy Before Surgery

Every muscle in your body is anchored to at least two bones. On either side of your back, a latissimus dorsi muscle attaches to the lower six chest (thoracic) vertebrae, the lower back (lumbar) vertebrae, and the portion of the hip bone closest to the spine (iliac crest). The muscle tapers upward as it approaches the place where it is affixed to the underside of the bone in the upper arm (humerus) (see Figure 8.1).

Your lat allows your shoulder to rotate and helps keep the wing bone (scapula) lying flat on your back. You use your lat when reaching overhead and pulling downward, such as when closing the trunk of a car, doing the crawl stroke while swimming, or planting and pushing off from your poles in cross-country skiing. It also helps when you are pushing yourself up from a seated position.

FIGURE 8.1 Back Muscles: Latissimus Dorsi

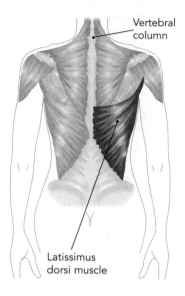

Vertebral column

Latissimus dorsi muscle

The latissimus dorsi (lat) muscle stretches from the lower spine and hip bone to an area on the upper arm behind your armpit.

Anatomy After Surgery

During lat flap surgery, the entire muscle, the fat above it, and a section of skin over the fat are rotated from the back to the chest wall. The surgeon first makes an elliptical skin incision shaped like an eye on your back. This can be horizontal, vertical, or diagonal. He or she then releases the muscle with its overlying fat and skin from its attachments to the spine and hip bone. The blood supply to the muscle comes from the *thoracodorsal artery*, which branches off from the *axillary artery* under the arm. These blood vessels and the portion of the lat muscle normally attached to the underside of the arm bone near the armpit are left intact. That ensures a good blood supply to keep muscle and tissue alive and healthy (see Figure 8.2).

Next, the surgeon creates a tunnel in the underarm area. Skin and fat lie on top of the tunnel, and the muscles at the side of the

FIGURE 8.2 Lat Flap

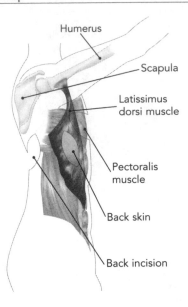

Humerus

Scapula

Latissimus
dorsi muscle

Pectoralis
muscle

Back skin

Back incision

The lat muscle is detached from the spine and hip bone. It remains connected to the humerus near the underarm. The muscle, along with the skin and fat above it, is then tunneled beneath the skin along the side of the body and repositioned on the chest to form the breast mound.

chest lie underneath it. The lat muscle is then rotated from the back, through the tunnel, onto the front of the chest, where it is repositioned to form the breast mound. Now the muscle is on the front of the body.

Usually, the lat muscle is not thick enough to be used alone to recreate a breast that matches its twin. Thus, the upper edge of the lat and the lower edge of the pectoral muscles are sewn together to form a pocket into which a permanent implant can be placed to add volume (see Figure 8.3).

Drains to siphon off the lymphatic fluid that accumulates after surgery are placed under the skin at the incision sites in the chest and back. The skin edges from the chest wall are then sewn to the skin edges from the lat flap. Finally, the incision on the back is sewn closed, too.

FIGURE 8.3 Lat Flap with Implant

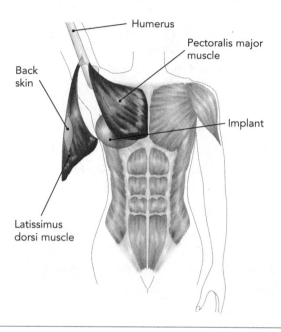

Generally the lat flap provides a small amount of tissue, so an additional implant often is needed. The edges of the lat and pectoral muscles of the chest are stitched together to create a pocket for the permanent implant.

The Challenges

Certain activities and tasks may become more difficult, though not necessarily impossible, after lat flap surgery, which may affect posture, flexibility, strength, and energy in the following ways.

How Is Posture Affected?

Joints in the body are stabilized by surrounding muscles, tendons, and ligaments. Good posture depends on the counterbalancing forces of chest wall muscles (pectoralis major and pectoralis minor) pulling the shoulder forward while the latissimus dorsi and other back muscles pull it backward. Now that the lat muscle is no longer in place, less backward force is being exerted.

Massage Therapy

Noticeable tightness from the pull of the muscle in its new location and from the back incision where skin is snugly sewn together can affect posture and shoulder flexibility. Sometimes that tightness—which some women liken to a thick band on a very tight sports bra—makes it hard to breathe deeply and comfortably. These sensations are common during the initial recovery period and may persist beyond it.

Scar tissue at the surgical sites may pucker and pull uncomfortably. Sometimes *cording*, a phenomenon in which muscle tendons or larger lymphatic channels stick to the under-surface of skin, occurs as scar tissue forms where underarm lymph nodes were removed or at surgical incision sites. When a woman lifts her arm, the skin in the underarm area pulls the muscle outward and a vertical cord can be seen.

Massage therapy by a trained physical therapist or massage therapist may be needed to ease tightness, release cording and scar tissue, and help regain shoulder mobility. Your plastic surgeon can evaluate you to see if this would help you heal. Information on finding an experienced physical therapist or massage therapist appears in Chapter 1.

Protective posturing—head tilted forward, shoulder raised and hunched, elbow bent so that your hand rests across your belly, and body bending forward at the waist—can occur because of discomfort after surgery and from tightness on your chest where the lat muscle is pulling in its new location and at your back incision where skin, fat, and muscle were removed.

How Is Flexibility Affected?

Flexibility—that is, the range of motion through which you can comfortably move a joint like your shoulder—is affected in several ways. Pain and discomfort from surgery can cause you to voluntarily limit your range of motion. Yet what starts as a temporary way to dodge discomfort may become permanent unless you begin to gently expand these limits. One example is a frozen shoulder, which stems from severely limiting your range of motion in your shoulder and arm for a prolonged time after surgery. Tightness in the joint results and worsens until normal movements become acutely painful.

The loss of the lat muscle in its usual position on the back keeps you from moving your shoulder freely. After the surgical sites heal, scar tissue also may interfere with free movement, too.

Stretching exercises—if necessary, coupled with massage therapy (see sidebar, "Massage Therapy") or physical therapy that may include heat, massage, passive stretches, and specific exercises—will help you regain a comfortable range of motion. If you had radiation therapy, it's particularly important to continue doing stretches regularly because skin and deep tissue changes due to radiation may affect flexibility for many months after treatment is finished.

How Are Muscles and Activities Affected?

Normally, the lat muscle allows you to turn your arm and rotate your shoulder forward (internal rotation) so that your thumb points to your body and your palm faces backward. It also permits you to lower an outstretched arm back down to your side (adduction). Some examples of activities that might be affected are:

- Pushing yourself up out of a chair, car, or bathtub
- Removing a box from a high shelf
- Closing the trunk or hatchback of your car or a garage door
- Pulling yourself up, such as when climbing a ladder
- Certain sports such as cross-country skiing, cycling (uphill), tennis or other racquet sports, rowing, kayaking, rock climbing
- Some strokes while swimming, such as the front crawl and butterfly
- Performing a lat pull-down on exercise machines at the gym

How Is Energy Affected?

Fatigue is a potent side effect of surgery. It follows on the heels of radiation and chemotherapy, too. As your body heals, it channels energy toward repairing and rebuilding cells. It's common for fatigue to last four to six weeks after radiation treatment, according to the National Cancer Institute (NCI). Dips in red blood cells stemming from certain chemotherapy drugs may make fatigue vary from week to week. Many women find their exhaustion snowballs as treatment proceeds. Other medical and emotional issues also may play a role. Discuss persistent exhaustion with your doctor, who can help identify root problems and suggest solutions. Some small, preliminary studies suggest light to moderate walking or other activities helps boost energy in those coping with cancer.

How Can I Help My Body Recover?

To recover as fully as possible, you need to regain comfortable upright posture, establish balance in flexibility and strength on both sides, and recruit muscles that can compensate for the loss of the lat. Rebuilding energy and endurance is essential, too. Each element of our program will help you move forward at a gradual pace. Posture checks and stretching are very important after lat flap surgery. Walking and balance exercises are key, as well. Strength exercises will help you regain lost ground. Chapters 9 through 12 contain information on when to begin exercising and how to exercise safely as well as the actual workouts.

Recovery from lat flap surgery may take a while, especially if you are also undergoing chemotherapy. Usually it takes three to six weeks before strength and energy improve enough for you to begin returning to most activities, though it may be longer before you truly feel like yourself.

When Can I Begin Exercising?

Obtain your surgeon's permission before you start our exercise program or add new exercises. Review the exercises you plan to do and discuss any limitations, such as not reaching above shoulder height during the early healing phase.

Make sure you understand the tips for exercising safely explained in Chapter 9. You'll find exercises, workouts, and a plan for getting started in Chapters 10 through 12. The right timing for beginning to exercise varies depending on the speed of your recovery and the advice of your surgeon.

Typically, you'll be encouraged to start walking the day after your surgery. Usually, activities that do not require you to lift your arm higher than shoulder height are safe at this point, too. Within two to four weeks, your surgeon may permit you to start the balance exercises, and between weeks three to six you may be able to add the stretching exercises as well. Once you can easily stand upright and have regained a full or comfortable range of motion, you should be able to begin our light strength-training exercises. Generally, this workout can be added around week 12.

CHAPTER 9

Exercise with Care

The well-designed workouts in this book have helped many breast cancer survivors. Selected and sequenced with your safety in mind, the exercises we chose are based upon recent breast cancer research and exercise guidelines from key sources such as the American College of Sports Medicine (ACSM) and recommendations made by government health experts. Our program is founded upon the best current health practices for women who have been treated for breast cancer and is approved by the American Council on Exercise (ACE).

Often, women have fears and misconceptions about exercising during their treatment or recovery. This chapter explains how to exercise safely and covers precautions for women concerned about lymphedema, swelling in soft tissue that occurs when lymph fluid backs up because lymph channels were altered by surgery or radiation. The sidebar "Save Your Shoulder" discusses how to tailor your exercise program to regain shoulder mobility and protect and strengthen your rotator cuff muscles. Additionally, we provide a list of necessary equipment and tools to help you establish a baseline for aerobic fitness, flexibility, balance, and strength so you can track your progress. Proper posture, which is essential to good form during exercise, is illustrated, too. Before you start exercising, make sure you read and understand this chapter.

Safety First

Safe exercising calls for common sense and some less obvious rules. Follow the "10 Basic Principles of Safety" outlined in this section as well as specific tips for stretching and strength-training exercises.

10 Basic Principles of Safety

1. **Get the go-ahead.** Discuss the workouts with your surgeon, who is best able to tell you if you should avoid or limit the range of motion of any exercises. She or he also can tell you whether the basic timeline provided in Chapter 10 will be right for you. Everyone heals differently, so this discussion is very important. If you haven't seen your surgeon in years, talk to your primary care physician. If you take any medications, check with the doctor who prescribed these, too. Some medications, such as beta-blockers, slow your heartbeat. Certain anticancer drugs, such as anastrozole (Arimidex), may make joints or muscles sore. Other medications, such as drugs for allergies, colds, high blood pressure, or diabetes, may affect vision or balance or make dehydration more likely to occur. Adjusting the dose or time when you take medication, if your doctor recommends this, or simply being aware of possible problems will help you exercise safely. Sometimes, serious health or physical problems make it safest to work out under medical supervision or to work with an experienced physical therapist or personal trainer.

2. **Take necessary precautions.** If you have had lymph nodes removed or had radiation therapy directed to your underarm or collarbone areas, fully review "Lymphedema and Exercise" later in this chapter.

3. **Warm up.** Before you exercise or stretch, dance to a few songs on the radio or walk for 5 to 10 minutes. If this is too tiring right now, take a warm bath or shower before starting to exercise.

4. **Follow our sequence.** Use the sequence laid out in each workout unless your doctor, physical therapist, or personal

trainer experienced in working with women treated for breast cancer advises otherwise. We deliberately rotate muscle groups to avoid overtaxing muscles weakened by surgery or triggering a cycle of lymphedema in women who have had lymph nodes removed or treated with radiation. The exercises selected reflect current research and safety concerns, so it's best to avoid substitutions. You may know another way to do an abdominal crunch, for example, but the crunches we have chosen strengthen core muscles while avoiding compressing the spine.

5. **Proceed slowly.** Expect slow, gradual improvement. Everyone is different, so comparing yourself to others—or even to yourself on a better day or at an earlier time in your life—isn't helpful.

6. **Balance both sides of your body.** Always lift the same amount of weight with both sides instead of lifting a heavier weight on your stronger side. The amount of weight you comfortably can lift with your weaker side should determine which weight to use. Similarly, when stretching, your goal is to achieve a full range of motion on each side. Be patient—over time, you will notice improvements.

7. **Focus on quality.** Quality is more important than quantity. If you cannot do all the repetitions or hold a stretch as long as suggested, do what is possible. Focus on good form, move slowly, and remain in control throughout each move.

8. **Always stop if you feel pain!** Readjust your position and try again, making your movements smaller, if necessary, so that you stay in a comfortable, pain-free range of motion. If an exercise still hurts, stop doing it and ask your doctor for advice. (See sidebar "Remember *RICE*" for information on treating a pulled or strained muscle.)

9. **Take time off, if necessary.** If you have a fever or are feeling especially fatigued or unwell, skip your exercise session and take the day off.

10. **Cool down.** After each walking or strength-training session, cool down for 5 to 10 minutes. Walking slowly or doing stretches is a good way to achieve this.

Remember *RICE*

Slightly sore muscles are not uncommon when you begin to do new exercises or step up activity levels. Pain and swelling, however, are signs of injury that often accompany a pulled muscle. If this occurs, try *RICE*, which cuts down inflammation and swelling:

- R: *Rest* the injured region until it recovers (generally, you can continue activities that don't involve this muscle)
- I: *Ice* the injured region for 10 to 15 minutes several times a day (put ice on top of a compression bandage or another cloth, not directly on skin)
- C: *Compress* the injured region by applying an elastic bandage
- E: *Elevate* (raise) the injured area above your heart, if possible

Two days (48 hours) of RICE may be all that is needed to treat a pulled muscle. If pain is severe or persists, call your doctor for advice.

Lymphedema and Exercise

When it comes to lymphedema, it's safest to err on the side of caution even if some recommendations are not backed by strong research. A full discussion of lymphedema triggers, prevention tips, and treatment appears in Chapter 3. Here, we briefly describe the lymphatic system and focus only on exercise precautions. Discuss the list of precautions with your surgeon or doctor, who can help decide which tips are most important, depending on whether you are at high or low risk for lymphedema.

Lymph channels, or vessels, branch out through the body. Channels in your arms carry the watery fluid called lymph to larger channels in the underarm. These ultimately feed into the central circulatory system so that lymph fluid joins the bloodstream. When surgery or radiation alters underarm lymph channels, there may not be enough remaining channels to allow easy drainage of lymph. Fluid backs up and accumulates in the affected arm and hand and, less often, in the trunk of the body.

Exercise has benefits and drawbacks as far as lymphedema is concerned. When you exercise, muscles squeeze and relax in a milking motion that moves lymph fluid along. The calories pared off by exercise may help you lose unwanted pounds, a particular boon for overweight women because obesity is thought to raise the risk for lymphedema. Yet vigorous exercise and arm movements may increase the rate of blood flow and lymph production to the point where it overwhelms remaining lymph channels, creating fluid backup and starting the lymphedema cycle. Our gentle exercise program, which gradually progresses, aims to encourage widening of remaining lymph channels in the shoulder while tempering increased lymph flow to the arm so that arm vessels are not overtaxed.

Taking the following precautions for exercise sessions may help:

- **Wear compression garments.** Wear well-fitted arm and hand compression garments, such as a compression sleeve or bandages, during strength training and any activities calling for repetitive arm motions (such as raking, rowing, and racquet sports), no matter how short the duration of these activities. This is essential for women who have had lymphedema and should be considered by women at risk for it, as explained in Chapter 3. Appearance boutiques in hospitals and other shops that sell breast forms or durable medical goods often can fit you for these. You also can contact the National Lymphedema Network (800-541-3259 or lymph net.org) or the American Cancer Society (800-ACS-2345 or cancer.org) to learn about suppliers in your area.
- **Gain control.** Before you begin the light strength-training program, make sure any lymphedema swelling is under control. Consult with a lymphedema therapist if necessary (see Chapter 3).
- **Stay cool.** Choose cooler times of day to exercise outdoors to avoid overheating, which may contribute to lymphedema.
- **Warm up.** Gently warm up muscles before starting to exercise.
- **Practice moderation.** Avoid long spans of repetitive, vigorous movements against resistance with the affected arm, such

as pushing or pulling, and limit sports with forceful, repetitive arm strokes.

- **Follow the sequence.** *This is essential.* By following the sequence laid out in our strength-training program, you will alternate upper body exercises with work on your core or legs. Each time you return to arm exercises, you will work on a different muscle group. So if you first worked your biceps and then your abs, you might next move to triceps. This sequence builds in rest time recommended by the National Lymphedema Network (NLN) to help prevent lymph buildup. We further recommend adding a stretch after each strength exercise from your balance and stretches workout.
- **Rest between strength-training sessions.** Leave at least two days (48 hours) between strength-training sessions.
- **Be alert to changes.** Be aware of your body before and during activities, suggests the NLN. Note any changes in size, shape, tissue texture, soreness, heaviness, or firmness in vulnerable areas, such as your arm or torso. Lie down and raise your arm if it begins to ache or swell or feels tight or heavy. This allows gravity to gently aid in sending fluid back toward the center of your body. Take additional steps advised by your doctor or a physical therapist or a professional trained in manual lymphatic drainage (see Resources).

The Toolbox

Simple equipment to help you get started is described in this section. A posture check and easy tests to help you establish a baseline for cardiovascular fitness, flexibility, and balance follow. You can use these tests monthly to track your progress. Filling in the exercise logs provided in Chapter 10 helps you track your progress as well.

Equipment

Only a handful of the tools you need for these workouts cost money. Others already are in your home. It's fine to start with the basics and add equipment as you progress in your workouts. For

Save Your Shoulder

Four muscles (the supraspinatus, infraspinatus, teres minor, and subscapularis) work in concert to form the rotator cuff, a small section of your shoulder that allows you to rotate your arm as well as to move it toward or away from your body. Often, breast cancer surgery—and especially reconstructive options like implant surgery and lat flap surgery—affect the rotator cuff, sparking pain at the shoulder, limiting range of motion, and making many tasks difficult to do. For example, it may be hard to lift an item overhead, retrieve a gallon of milk from the top shelf in the refrigerator, open and close doors, reach behind yourself, or throw a ball.

Many of the exercises in this book are designed to help you regain shoulder mobility and strengthen your rotator cuff muscles. The workout plans tailored to the type of surgery you've had include a variety of these exercises. If you had a mastectomy, traditional lymph node surgery (see Chapter 3), or breast reconstruction, you will benefit from an exercise regimen designed to further help to rehabilitate the rotator cuff.

Restoring shoulder range of motion is absolutely essential *before* you begin to do strength-training exercises. Carefully adding shoulder warm-ups and stretches to your daily routine will help you to do this. Start with the warm-ups listed below under Phase I. Once you can do these easily and comfortably, move to the Phase II stretches if your doctor

and "The Right Timing" chart in Chapter 10 agree that it is time to start stretches. When you become accomplished at Phase II stretches, you will be ready to move to Phase III. For example, if you are comfortably doing the Butterfly Stretch, you are ready to progress when you can touch both arms to the floor. If you're still using pillows under your arms, give yourself more time to work on this.

Phase I: Warm-Ups

- Shoulder Pendulum, 10 times, once or twice a day (page 144)
- Shoulder Circles, 10 times, once or twice a day (page 145)

Phase II: Stretches

- Single Arm Overhead Stretch, 2–4 times on each side, once or twice a day (page 152)
- Wall Climb: Front, 2–4 times on each side, once or twice a day (page 153)
- Wall Climb: Side, 2–4 times on each side, once or twice a day (page 154)
- Butterfly Stretch, 2–4 times, once or twice a day (page 155)

Phase III: Warm Up and Stretch

- Scapula Squeezes, 10 times, once or twice a day (page 146)
- Single Arm Wall Stretch, 2–4 times on each side, once or twice a day (page 159)

(continued)

Save Your Shoulder, *continued*

When to Start Strength Training

Even if "The Right Timing" chart suggests that it's time to start strength training, you should hold off until you can comfortably do the three phases of warm-ups and stretches described. When you have reached that point and have gotten permission from your doctor, you are ready to start the Save Your Shoulder Strength Workout in Chapter 12.

- Begin with the Save Your Shoulder Strength Workout Phase 1. Your goal is to be able to do two sets of 10 repetitions. Start with just one set (and, if necessary, fewer repetitions). Gradually build up to the goal of two sets of 10 repetitions as you progress.
- When you accomplish this, you are ready to move on to the Save Your Shoulder Strength Workout Phase 2. Once you can do two sets of 10 repetitions of these exercises, you are ready to progress to the Chapter 12 strength workouts tailored for the type of surgery you had.

Additional Safety Tips

We strongly recommend enhancing shoulder range of motion and strength under the guidance of a physical therapist or personal trainer experienced in working with breast cancer survivors who can choose the best exercises for you based on your needs. It is essential to add on carefully and to follow these tips to minimize injury:

- *Warm up properly.* Warm-up exercises in the preceding list can be performed daily.
- *Stretch slowly and comfortably.* The stretches listed can be added to your Stretch and Balance workout. They should be performed after you warm up. When

example, you needn't buy hand weights and resistance tubes until you are ready to start strength training.

You'll need:

- Well-cushioned walking shoes
- A basic pedometer
- A set of resistance tubes or bands, preferably with handles
- Light hand weights (one-pound, two-pound, three-pound, and five-pound hand weights at first, then heavier weights as you grow stronger)

stretching, your goal is to achieve the maximum pain-free range of motion possible for you. Do stretches slowly to allow soft tissues to lengthen.

- *Maintain good form.* Control and good form are essential during any exercise and especially so during strength training. The number of repetitions per set specified for each exercise is merely a goal. If necessary, do fewer repetitions initially to maintain control and good form. Add repetitions gradually as you progress. For strength training, do only as many repetitions as possible while controlling the movement and maintaining good form.
- *Rest between strength sessions.* Strength exercises require a 48-hour rest between sessions to allow muscles to recover.
- *Stay safe.* Follow safety precautions described throughout this chapter especially in "Lymphedema and Exercise," if

you have had lymph nodes removed or radiation to the underarm or collarbone area. Also review Chapter 3, if so. If you experience pain or other limitations while performing your exercises, work with a physical therapist or personal trainer with expertise in this area to avoid injury and regain flexibility and strength.

- *Listen to your body.* Stop if you feel any pain!

If you currently feel shoulder pain or are having trouble moving your arm or shoulder freely, do not perform any strength exercises for the rotator cuff or attempt to work on the problem yourself. Instead, have a physical therapist evaluate your shoulder and prescribe a workout plan. Talk to your doctor first if you need a referral. Information on finding experienced physical therapists and personal trainers

- Weight-lifting gloves (optional)
- An exercise mat (optional)
- A sturdy stability ball (optional)
- A small towel
- Pillows
- A water bottle

When buying equipment, look for a sporting goods store that has a good selection in various price ranges (see Resources, also). Try on several pairs of walking shoes to see which are most comfortable and provide the best support for your feet. Lift a few different types of light hand weights. Weights with a padded center bar are more comfortable to grip. Those with a smooth coating (or bare metal) can become slippery as you perspire. D-shaped padded weights work well for women with arthritis who have trouble gripping. Weights that screw onto a center bar save space in your home, although you may find it cumbersome to add and subtract weights during exercise sessions as you progress. Usually, iron dumbbells are least expensive. Resale shops for exercise equipment often have weights at low prices. In a pinch, soup cans make fine starter weights.

Posture Check

Few of us can boast perfect posture. Pain and tenderness after surgery often compound already questionable habits of slouching and poor alignment. The resulting imbalances affect your ability to perform exercises correctly—that is, with good form—which can lead to injuries. Over time, imbalances and poor posture often snowball into back, neck, and knee pain, too.

Check yourself in a mirror to see how your posture measures up to the illustrations in Figures 9.1 and 9.2. We recommend doing this regularly as part of your exercise program. Apply the following tips when you walk, stretch, or do other exercises, too.

Neutral position—a term used by exercise experts—essentially means not deliberately tilted forward or backward. When your wrist is in a neutral position, for example, you hold it firm and straight as a pipe. Your spine has natural curves even when in a neutral position. Keeping your hip bones in line over your pubic bone, rather than tipping your pelvis forward or backward, will help you hold your spine in a neutral position. Good *alignment* is important, too. That means shoulders even and hips even. As you look downward, you should notice that your knees, ankles, and toes fall in a line, regardless of whether your feet are together or apart.

FIGURE 9.1 Posture: Front

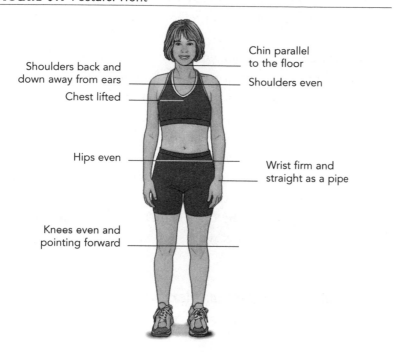

Shoulders back and down away from ears

Chest lifted

Hips even

Knees even and pointing forward

Chin parallel to the floor

Shoulders even

Wrist firm and straight as a pipe

FIGURE 9.2 Posture: Side

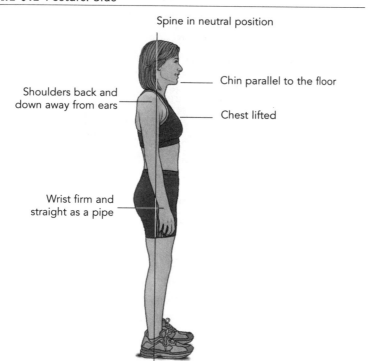

Spine in neutral position

Shoulders back and down away from ears

Chin parallel to the floor

Chest lifted

Wrist firm and straight as a pipe

Establish Your Baseline: Walking

You can decide whether you prefer to count minutes or steps.

- **Minutes.** How long are you able to walk without tiring? Go out for a walk on three days, counting minutes each time. Add the totals and divide by three to reach your average. This is your baseline.

    Minutes baseline: _____
- **Steps.** Clip your pedometer onto your hip when you get up in the morning and wear it all day to record your total number of steps. Over the course of three days, add up your total steps per day. Divide by three to get the average number of steps. This is your baseline.

    Steps baseline: _____

Establish Your Baseline: Flexibility

Once your surgeon has given you permission to begin the stretches in our program, you can perform a baseline assessment of your range of motion. It is ideal to do so before you have surgery, if possible, because you'll more easily spot changes in your range of motion afterward. If this isn't possible, assess the side on which you had surgery against your other side. Perform the following stretches on both sides of your body.

- **Wall Climb: Front.** (See instructions, page 153.) Put a mark or piece of tape on the wall to show how high you reached, then measure in inches from the floor. Also note how far away from the wall you are standing.

    Left baseline: _____
    Distance away from wall: _____
    Right baseline: _____
    Distance away from wall: _____
- **Wall Climb: Side.** (See instructions, page 154.) Place a mark or piece of tape on the wall to show how high you reached, then measure that off in inches. Also note how far away from the wall you are standing.

Left baseline: _____

    Distance away from wall:_____

Right baseline: _____

    Distance away from wall:_____

Establish Your Baseline: Balance

Safety is the first consideration when establishing your balance baseline. Be prepared to hold onto a counter or the back of a chair if you lose your balance. When you are ready, perform the Single Leg Stance (see instructions, page 151) on each leg. See if you are able to balance more easily on one side than on the other. Time yourself standing on each foot for up to 60 seconds.

Left baseline: _____

Right baseline: _____

Establish Your Baseline: Strength

Before you establish a baseline for strength, check Table 10.1, "The Right Timing," in Chapter 10 and discuss when to start strength training with your surgeon. Read the information about strength training in Chapter 10, too, so that you'll be able to work out safely. Strength workouts tailored to each type of surgery can be found in Chapter 12.

We recommend performing the exercises without weights for at least a few sessions. Wait to set a strength baseline until it becomes easy to do 10 repetitions of each exercise with proper form and a full or comfortable range of motion. At that point, you can begin to use light weights.

To set your strength baseline, write down the exercises in your workout plan. Start by performing 10 repetitions of the first exercise in your workout with a light weight (one to three pounds). Focus on good form and a full or comfortable range of motion throughout. The last few repetitions should require moderate effort. If 10 repetitions with one to three pounds is too easy, then pick up a heavier weight and repeat the exercise until you find the amount of weight that requires moderate effort on the last few repetitions. This will be your baseline.

If two or three pounds is too hard, set your baseline at one pound. If that is too hard, do not use any weight at all. Simply go through the movement. Repeat this process for all of the strength exercises in your workout.

Strength Baseline		
Exercise	Repetitions (up to 10)	Weight

CHAPTER 10

A Plan for Every Woman

The right mix of exercises and the right timing for getting started are outlined in this chapter. Scales that will help you work out at a safe level of intensity are described here, too. You also will find sample exercise logs to copy and fill in as you launch your work-outs. Although general principles remain the same for every woman, the exercises and timing chosen for the workout plans vary depending on the extent of your surgery and the speed of your recovery. Discuss this with your doctor.

The Right Mix

Over the course of a week, a comprehensive exercise plan combines cardiovascular training with balance, stretching, and strength exercises. If the thought of all this exhausts you, take heart: you'll start to build toward this slowly and add on as you feel ready to progress.

Slow progress is best because it allows your heart, lungs, mus-cles, skin, and other tissues to gradually adapt to challenges pre-sented by the exercises. Even women starting this program many years after their treatment will find a gradual approach valuable, particularly if they have not been active.

Often, women feel exhausted at various times during treat-ment and recovery, especially in the weeks after surgery or during the course of chemotherapy or radiation therapy. If your energy fluctuates, try to take a walk or do other activities at times of day when you feel least tired. A little exercise is always better than none. Think of activity as a bank—add small amounts several times a day by taking a short walk or doing a group of balance exercises or stretches so that the final tally rises gradually. On days or at times when you feel better, try to do more; on difficult days, accept that you need to do less or sometimes even take the day off. Ultimately, the workouts we've selected will help energize you while easing aches and pains.

Cardiovascular Exercise

After surgery, the very first thing you can do for yourself is get out of bed and walk. Usually, it's fine to do so by the second day. Make sure that someone walks alongside you to assist you as necessary. The first steps you take may simply be the short path from bed to bathroom. Next, try to walk to the nurses' station, and then to the end of the hall. Rather than concentrating on speed, focus on traveling a little bit farther each time. It takes time, but by walking as often as you can, you will gradually attain goals that seem completely out of reach right now—whether that is a short walk without pain or a much longer walk at a pace you enjoy.

If you follow health news, you know that goalposts for cardiovascular exercise sometimes shift confusingly. Our guidelines—and thus, your goals—stem from careful analysis of numerous sources, including recent breast cancer research, the 2005 Dietary Guidelines for Americans, and recommendations made for cancer patients by the American College of Sports Medicine. Our simple walking program delivers significant benefits that vary depending on the time expended:

- **Breast cancer benefits.** Walking at an average pace for three to five hours a week (about 30 minutes a day) cuts the risk for breast cancer recurrence by 40 percent, according to data from the Nurses' Health Study published in 2005.
- **Additional health benefits.** Walking for 30 minutes most days of the week offers health benefits, such as lowering

Cardiovascular Benefits of Walking

Simply put, regular walks are better for your all-around health than many medications. What's more, walking is far less costly and has no significant side effects. Engaging in a walking program on most days of the week delivers a multitude of benefits, including these:

- Cuts breast cancer recurrence and may improve survival among women who have been treated for breast cancer.
- Burns off calories, which helps in weight loss and maintaining a healthy weight, and pares down fat cells. Fat cells produce estrogen, so having fewer fat cells may be advantageous for women whose breast cancers are fueled by estrogen.

- Lowers risks for heart disease, high blood pressure, diabetes, and several types of cancer.
- May make it possible to take less medication for certain health problems, such as high blood pressure, high cholesterol, diabetes, and even pain.
- Helps maintain bone strength in the lower body because walking is a weight-bearing activity (unlike some other cardiovascular activities, such as swimming and cycling).
- Boosts mood and eases anxiety and mild depression.
- Improves sleep.

your risk for heart disease, diabetes, osteoporosis, and many other ailments, according to the 2005 Dietary Guidelines for Americans.

- **Healthy weight benefits.** Weight matters to good health, too, and may play a role in survival after breast cancer treatment, as explained in Chapter 2. Combined with a healthy diet, walking 30 to 60 minutes on most days of the week can help keep you from gaining weight. Raising the bar to 60 to 90 minutes most days of the week may be necessary if you're struggling to lose weight or have lost a great deal and wish to keep those pounds from creeping back. Our bodies and our eating habits differ, so you'll need to see what works best for you. See Chapters 1 and 2 for more information if you are trying to lose weight.

Setting Goals. Here are tips to help you set your goals for walking.

- **Frequency.** Start out walking at least three times a week. Work up to most days or daily if possible.
- **Intensity.** Start at 1 on the effort scale (see sidebar, "Measuring Intensity: Scales and Songs"). Move to 2 or 3 on the effort scale as you feel able to do so. Initially, adding days and time or steps is more important than boosting intensity.
- **Progressing.** First add days until you are walking as many days of the week as possible. Next, set new goals by adding time or steps to your baseline assessment in Chapter 9. Some days you won't be able to reach your goal—you may even slip backward. Remember that any activity is better than none. On other days you will exceed your goal. Keep trying!
  - **Counting time?** To progress, add at least 10 percent to your baseline to set a new goal. Thus, if your baseline is 10 minutes, add 1 minute so that your new goal is 11 minutes. Depending on how fast you feel able to move ahead, you could add 10 percent to your current goal daily, twice a week, or once a week. Each time you do this, you set a new goal for yourself. Ultimately, aim for 30 to 60 minutes of walking during the day, which can be divided into 10- or 15-minute segments.
  - **Tracking steps with a pedometer?** Clip it onto your hip as soon as you get up in the morning. Each day, try to add 10 percent more steps than the previous day's walk. Thus, if your baseline is 500 steps, you'll add 50 steps (10 percent) to 500 steps for a total of 550 steps. The following day, try adding 55 steps plus 550 steps for a total of 605 steps and so on. As your walking program progresses, make your intermediate goals 3,000 steps, 6,000 steps, and 8,000 steps. Ultimately, aim for 10,000 steps a day.
- **Having trouble?** Are these goals too daunting? They may seem unattainable if you recently have had surgery, are undergoing chemotherapy or radiation, or simply haven't been physically active before. If so, make walking 5 minutes every hour your first goal. At the end of eight hours, you'll

have walked 40 minutes. Gradually build up to longer walks. If a goal you set proves too hard, listen to your body and just do what you can on as many days of the week as possible.

Starting Off. A few tips before you start:

- **Get ready.** Go to the bathroom. For cool weather, dress for outdoor walks in layers of clothes to peel off as needed. Put on sunscreen and a broad-brimmed hat. Fill up your water bottle and plan to sip from it often to stay hydrated.
- **Stay safe.** Walk with a partner if possible, especially at first. Have a destination in mind, but listen to your body so that you rest or stop when you need to do so. Carry a cell phone, identification, and phone numbers. If you're walking on a road, traffic should be coming toward you.
- **Warm up.** Walk slowly for five minutes. The swing of your arms dictates your pace. Once you've warmed up, move more quickly, if possible (see sidebar, "Measuring Intensity: Scales and Songs").
- **Practice good posture.** Check your posture and alignment occasionally as you walk:
  - Keep your chin parallel to the ground.
  - Lift your chest and roll your shoulders back and down away from your ears, then relax them.
  - Pull in your abdominal muscles.
  - Swing your arms forward and backward in a relaxed fashion. (Do not swing your arms from side to side as if rocking a baby.)
  - Stride comfortably and naturally, planting the heel, ball, and then toe of your foot.
  - Breathe normally.
- **Cool down.** Walk slowly for five minutes.

Stretching Exercises

Gentle stretching exercises go hand in hand with the early weeks of your walking program. All of our stretch and balance workouts are tailored to the type of surgery you've undergone.

Measuring Intensity: Scales and Songs

How intensely should you exercise? Since this is a beginner's program, we recommend a gentle pace at first. As you get stronger and build more endurance, you can start to step it up. You can measure intensity in a few ways.

Effort and Fatigue Scales

These simple scales measure your perception of how intensely you are working out. The scales take into account personal variations in fitness and ups and downs in energy that are typical during treatment and recovery. For example, you might consider it a breeze to walk six blocks, feeling that this requires an easy effort on your part that is mildly fatiguing. Only if you walked much faster or up hills would your effort and fatigue scales creep higher. A woman less fit—or tuckered out by treatment—may find six blocks at a slow pace requires a hard effort and leaves her feeling very fatigued.

Effort Scale

0 = No effort
1 = Easy effort
2 = Moderate effort
3 = Hard effort
4 = Working too hard

Fatigue Scale

0 = No fatigue
1 = Mild fatigue
2 = Moderate fatigue
3 = Very fatigued
4 = Exhausted

When you start walking or adding other new activities, you should feel that you are working around number 1 on the effort scale. As you progress, it's fine to aim for number 2 or 3 on the effort scale. If you're heading toward number 4—working too hard—it is crucial to listen to your body and take a rest.

Energy fluctuates during treatment and recovery. If you feel you are at 3 or 4 on the fatigue scale (very fatigued or exhausted), give yourself permission to take a day off and rest.

Talking and Singing

As your heartbeat and breathing quicken, talking becomes harder. If you can sing, try to pick up your pace. If you're breathing comfortably and talking fairly normally, you're doing fine for a beginner. As you progress past the beginner stage, start to pick up the pace. Anytime you're too out of breath to manage short sentences, slow down a bit.

Why is stretching so essential? It counters stiffness and changes in posture that follow surgery and sometimes radiation. Otherwise, inactivity can permit muscles and tendons to shorten and

Minute by Minute, Step by Step, Mile by Mile

How do minutes stack up to steps, and where do miles fit in? When you're up to the challenge, these guidelines are useful:

Minutes and Miles

Measure a mile of city blocks (roughly 20 blocks) or country lanes with the odometer in a car. Then see how long it takes you to walk that distance:

- 20 minutes = 3 miles per hour
- 17 minutes, 10 seconds = 3.5 miles per hour
- 15 minutes = 4 miles per hour
- 13 minutes, 20 seconds = 4.5 miles per hour

Steps and Miles

Step measurements are more approximate because strides differ from person to person:

- 2,000 steps = 1 mile
- 4,000 steps = 2 miles
- 6,000 steps = 3 miles
- 8,000 steps = 4 miles
- 10,000 steps = 5 miles

If you'd like to be more exact, use the odometer in a car to measure off a mile, then count your steps with a pedometer and make up your own mile chart.

tighten in less than ideal positions. After TRAM surgery, for example, it's natural to bend forward at the waist and hip to avoid pain and tension at the broad abdominal incision where skin and muscle were taken from the belly and moved up to the chest. Over time, this can shorten the hip flexors that link legs to trunk, making it hard to straighten the legs and causing lower back pain. What's more, such decreased flexibility prompts lasting problems with posture and balance and may interfere with daily tasks.

Stretching is the first step toward regaining flexibility—that is, the ability to move each joint through its range of motion with little resistance from surrounding muscles and tissues. Not only will our program make you more flexible—in fact, probably more so than you were before surgery—it improves posture and balance, enabling you to undertake daily tasks and activities with minimal effort and maximum effect.

Stretching Benefits

Along with benefits already mentioned, stretching:

- Helps you regain full range of motion in joints.
- Relaxes stiff muscles and tight skin so that blood flows more easily, shuttling nutrients into these tissues and flushing away toxins.
- Gives you the ability to realign muscles and joints to improve posture and balance.
- Makes muscles more elastic and less prone to injury. If part of your treatment plan includes radiation therapy, stretching will enable you to more comfortably raise your arm and hold it in position during radiation sessions.

- Lubricates and protects joints by increasing the amount of synovial fluid, a natural lubricant that cushions joints. This helps prevent joint injury and degeneration, which can lead to arthritis.
- Enhances body awareness by helping you focus on how each muscle or muscle group moves and feels as you stretch.
- Improves coordination by reducing muscle resistance and helping your body adapt to moving in many directions.
- Enables you to more quickly counter sudden shifts in balance and thus makes falls less likely.
- Promotes relaxation and eases stress by relieving nervous tension and calming body and mind.

Setting Goals. Here are tips to help you set your goals for practicing stretching exercises.

- **Frequency.** Repeat each stretch 2–4 times, once or twice a day.
- **Intensity.** Only stretch to the point of tightness.
- **Time.** Hold each stretch 5–20 seconds (or longer, if you like, since after 20 seconds you may feel the muscle relax further).
- **Progressing.** The more often you perform the stretches, the more quickly your body will regain a comfortable range of motion.

Our program is designed to enhance recovery from surgery, so it differs slightly from guidelines issued by the American College of Sports Medicine (ACSM) in 2006. We recommend performing stretches once or twice a day, while the ACSM recommends doing stretches at least two to three times a week (and ideally five to seven times). Because your body is recovering from surgery, we recommend holding stretches for 5–20 seconds, while the ACSM recommends 15–30 seconds. Hold each stretch at the point of tightness without discomfort other than that which you might normally feel after surgery.

Starting Off. A few tips before you start:

- **Get the go-ahead.** Find out from your surgeon whether you need to limit your range of motion or avoid certain stretches at first. A doctor may recommend not raising your arms above shoulder level for a number of weeks after surgery, especially if you had reconstructive surgery. Show your surgeon the stretches in your workout so that she or he can decide what is best for you.
- **Warm up.** Muscles are like bubble gum—when warm, they stretch farther and more easily and are less likely to tear or be injured. Before performing a stretching workout, warm your muscles for at least 5–10 minutes by walking, dancing to a few songs, engaging in exercise, or taking a warm bath or shower.
- **Proceed slowly.** Start slowly and build gradually, progressing at your own pace. Over time, making the effort to stretch correctly and consistently while focusing on problem areas will loosen your muscles, improve your flexibility, and make you feel better. As a quick illustration of these benefits, try this: Slowly turn your head to the point of tightness. Hold the position for 5–20 seconds, breathing normally. Slowly turn back to center. Repeat three times. Do you notice a difference in how far you can comfortably turn?
- **Stay in control.** Make smooth, controlled movements, stretching just to the point of tightness. When you feel com-

fortable, see if you can take the stretch a little bit farther. Don't strain to hold any pose. Think of bending a finger back toward your wrist until you begin to feel a stretch. If you push farther, you'll start to feel pain. Similarly, as you stretch other muscles in your body, you want to feel the stretch without feeling pain.

- **Listen to your body.** Muscle fibers stretched too far spark pain. In response, nerves tell your muscles to contract. This *stretch reflex* helps prevents injury. Some discomfort is realistic after surgery, but pushing a stretch too far or bouncing does more harm than good. Your muscles actually tighten to protect themselves rather than relaxing. Overstretching temporarily or permanently damages muscle fibers, prompting increased soreness and the formation of scar tissue that can further affect flexibility.
- **Hold and relax.** Usually, we recommend holding stretches for 5–20 seconds. If you wish to hold a stretch a bit longer, do so. After 20 seconds you may feel the muscle relax further, so holding for up to 30 seconds can pay more dividends.
- **Breathe deeply.** Breathe smoothly in through your nose and out through your mouth. Deep, fluid breathing relaxes you, thereby improving the effectiveness of each stretch.

Balance Exercises

As we go about our lives, many of us give little thought to balance—the ability to respond to challenges to our equilibrium while standing still (*static balance*) or moving (*dynamic balance*). Your center of gravity hovers over the center of your legs to maintain balance. That sounds easy, but it is really quite complex. Sensory systems—among them vision, hearing, and special receptor cells in skin, muscle, joints, tendons, and ligaments called proprioceptors—collect information about your body as you move. Your brain processes these signals and sends motor commands to the appropriate parts of your body. Staying balanced requires your body to constantly adjust itself and quickly adapt to changes.

As we grow older, sensory receptors become less sensitive, so that the brain receives less information about the body's posi-

A PLAN FOR EVERY WOMAN

Balance Training Benefits

When done consistently, balance training:

- Counters some effects of skin tightness, muscle imbalances, and body asymmetry after breast surgery, which could otherwise throw off balance in ways that make even simple movements challenging or hazardous.
- Enhances stability, thus lessening the likelihood of falls. Falls are especially worrisome for older women, whose bones tend to be more fragile, and for breast cancer survivors, who are at higher than normal risk for bone thinning and, possibly, bone fractures due to chemotherapy and anticancer medications that affect bone density.
- Eases the fear of falling, which can be a potent barrier that gets in the way of daily tasks and enjoyable activities.
- Wakes up reflexes and improves control, coordination, gait, and posture while enhancing body awareness.

tion in space. Deteriorating eyesight, depth perception, and muscle strength coupled with slower reflexes further diminish equilibrium.

Whether balance is thrown off by surgery or age, compensating by taking smaller steps or standing with feet apart actually makes it harder to negotiate obstacles safely. A fall, or merely being anxious about falling, may encourage you to withdraw from daily activities and thus prompts a steady decline in your quality of life.

Balance training, which strengthens legs and improves flexibility in the feet, is often left out of exercise programs. Yet everyone can benefit from it, and women who have had breast cancer surgery, which can easily affect posture and balance, truly need it. Being off balance is a serious problem. If the wheels of a finely tuned car are badly balanced, unevenly worn tires, a bumpy ride, extra fuel demands, and loss of control that may lead to accidents typically follow. It's not all that different for humans. Spending just 5 to 10 minutes each day on balance training exercises can make a significant difference.

Setting Goals. Here are tips to help you set your goals for practicing balance training.

- **Frequency.** Repeat each balance exercise three to five times, once or twice a day.
- **Intensity.** Aim for 1 or 2 on the effort scale. These are gentle exercises.
- **Progressing.** The more often you do balance training, the better the results, so think about incorporating these easy exercises into your day—while standing at the sink, perhaps, talking on the phone, waiting at a store, or watching TV.

Starting Off. A few tips about balance and balance training before you start:

- **Check medications.** Some medications, such as sedatives, muscle relaxants, and blood pressure drugs, may cause weakness, dizziness, lightheadedness, or loss of balance. Certain chemotherapy drugs, such as paclitaxel (Taxol), can affect sensation in your feet and hands. Other medications taken during treatment can cause fatigue, diminish alertness, and impair judgment so that falls and other accidents occur. Particularly if you take four or more medications, some side effects, such as dizziness, are more likely to occur. Talk to your doctor about possible side effects from prescription and over-the-counter medications. Your doctor may be able to recommend substitute medications or a lower dose if you are experiencing problems, or can suggest other helpful precautions to take while exercising.
- **Stay hydrated.** Dizziness sometimes stems from dehydration, which may be hastened by drinking too little, heat, exercise, changes tied to aging, some medications like diuretics, and certain chemotherapy drugs. Make sure you take in enough fluids during the day. By the time you actually feel thirsty enough to crave a drink, you already may be somewhat dehydrated. Checking your urine (it should be straw-colored, not dark) usually is more helpful.

- **Check sight and glasses.** Poor vision may affect balance, so regular eye exams are a good idea. Regular eye exams are especially important for women taking tamoxifen (Nolvadex), a drug that slightly raises the risk of cataracts, which can blur vision. Be aware that bifocals and reading glasses can impair depth perception. Be careful if you wear them while exercising.

- **Prevent falls.** Throughout the day and especially while exercising, wear shoes that grip and provide proper support. Wear outfits that won't trip you by steering clear of clothes that are too big or too long. Clear away or avoid other household hazards, such as loose rugs or carpets, clutter, insufficient lighting, electrical cords, pets, spills, slippery floor surfaces, and the like.

- **Steady yourself.** Make it a habit to stabilize yourself before you move. Often people lose balance when they get up, change directions, or transfer their weight too quickly. Rising swiftly after sitting or lying down makes some people dizzy due to a sudden drop in blood pressure (*orthostatic hypotension*). If you're lying down, slowly sit up and wait a few moments before standing; if you're sitting, slowly get up.

- **Gain support.** When first starting to do balance exercises, stand next to a counter or a chair for support. Check your posture in the mirror before and during exercises. Square your shoulders and hips. Notice any imbalances. Becoming aware of strengths and weaknesses will help you to make improvements.

Strength Exercises

Strength training can benefit anyone, regardless of age, but is especially helpful for breast cancer survivors left with muscle imbalances and weaknesses after surgery. The muscles of your body can be likened to a rowing team. Pulling on the oars all together speeds the boat ahead. Uncoordinated actions by rowers slow the boat or simply do nothing to help advance it. If one rower is tired or drops off the team, the rest of the rowers must pick up the slack to reap the same results. Similarly, if you've had reconstructive surgery in which a muscle was relocated, you must recruit and strengthen surrounding muscles to compensate for the loss. If a muscle or muscle group has weakened due to surgery or inactivity, you must rebuild its strength gradually so that daily tasks and enjoyable activities become possible again.

One more among many reasons to begin strength training is findings from a study published in the journal *Cancer* in 2006. Eighty-six women who had been treated for breast cancer were randomly assigned to a group that performed weight training twice a week or a control group for six months. As upper body strength or muscle mass improved in the strength training group, so, too, did a variety of measures of psychosocial well-being. Physical challenges that disrupted daily activities eased, for example. Communication grew better in personal relationships and with medical team members.

Walking, balance training, and stretching all have a place in the early weeks after surgery. Strength training does not. Before you begin strength training:

- Work on regaining upright posture and a comfortable or full range of motion in your joints, especially at the shoulder.
- Wait until surgical drains have been removed and tissues have healed. You should have no open wounds from surgery or radiation therapy.
- Ask your surgeon whether your surgery (and reconstruction, if you had this) has healed sufficiently for you to start our light-weight training program.
- If you had a mastectomy, traditional lymph node surgery, or reconstructive surgery, also see the information in the "Save Your Shoulder" sidebar in Chapter 9. It explains how to tailor your exercise program to regain shoulder mobility and protect and strengthen shoulder rotator cuff muscles.

Pushing ahead too quickly before these conditions are met may set you up for serious injuries. It can hamper healing and affect the cosmetic outcome of reconstructive surgery.

Strength Training Benefits

When done consistently, strength exercises deliver many benefits, including these:

- Adds muscle, improving the muscle-to-fat ratio, which helps reverse changes prompted by chemotherapy, aging, or inactivity over time.
- Burns off a handful of extra calories every day if you add muscle through consistent, progressive strength training. (A pound of muscle burns twice as many calories as a pound of fat.) This may not make pounds melt away overnight, but every little bit counts.
- Helps preserve or, in some cases, strengthen bones throughout the body. That helps slow accelerated loss of bone density caused by chemotherapy, early menopause, side effects of certain anti-cancer drugs, or simply aging.

- Improves balance and posture, partly by building core strength. Also counters muscle imbalances tied to weakening of certain muscles on the side of the body affected by surgery or due to the relocation of a muscle with reconstructive surgery. These improvements make falls less likely.
- Adds to quality of life by making tasks and activities easier and more enjoyable, whether you're lifting a child or a bag of groceries or playing sports. During treatment and even for some time afterward, cancer can rob you of a sense of control. Strength training can empower you physically and mentally in ways that return control to you.

Setting Goals. Here are tips to help you set your goals for strength training.

- **Frequency.** Start with one set of strength exercises one or two times a week. Ultimately, aim for three times a week. Rest at least two days (48 hours) between sessions.
- **Intensity.** At first, aim for 1 on the effort scale. As you progress, work out at 2 or 3 on the scale. If lymphedema is a concern, ask your doctor about this before beginning our program.

- **Choosing weight.** Initially, do the exercises without any weights so you can focus on proper body alignment, a full or comfortable range of motion, and slow, steady, controlled movements. Next, choose a light weight of one to three pounds that makes you feel only mildly fatigued by the end of 10 repetitions. The amount of weight will vary depending on the exercise. A *repetition*, or *rep*, means going through the movement one time. In our program, 10 reps equals one *set*. You should be able to maintain good form, use a full, comfortable range of motion, and stay in control throughout all 10 reps. If not, decrease the weight.
- **Progressing.** When 10 reps become easy to do, you have some choices about how to progress. Change only one at a time:
  - Increase weight by the smallest amount possible (for example, go from one-pound to two-pound weights).
  - *Or*, increase sets (go from one set to two sets, or from two sets to three sets) by repeating the entire workout from start to finish.
  - *Or*, increase days (go from one to two days a week, or from two to three days a week). Be sure to rest for two days between sessions.

American College of Sports Medicine (ACSM) guidelines recommend two or three weekly strength training sessions during which you perform one to three sets of 8 to 10 exercises that overload—that is, tire out—the major muscles of the body. Because you are rebuilding strength after surgery, the program we suggest is lighter. If you feel especially tired, take a day off or cut back on the amount of weight you lift or the number of repetitions you perform.

Starting Off. A few tips before you start:

- **Check precautions.** If you have had lymph nodes removed or radiation treatments to the underarm or collarbone area,

Safe Soreness and Pain

Mild muscle soreness within 12 to 48 hours after strength training or another workout may occur. Don't worry that you've harmed yourself. After a day or two of rest from those activities, your muscles will repair themselves, becoming a bit stronger in the process, and the soreness will subside. If your joints feel sore, rather than your muscles, and this doesn't improve or go away within 72 hours, call your doctor for advice. Also, be aware that some anticancer medications may trigger marked muscle or joint soreness. "If I overdo it, I get chronic aches in the muscle," says Wendy Tompkins. She found temporarily cutting back on exercise and then moving ahead more slowly eased this.

A pulled muscle usually causes real pain, not soreness. Check the sidebar "Remember *RICE*" in Chapter 9 or call your doctor for advice.

review the lymphedema precautions for exercise in Chapter 9.

- **Choose a workout.** Review the "Save Your Shoulder" sidebar in Chapter 9 to see if you would benefit from a regimen designed to help you regain shoulder mobility and protect and strengthen your rotator cuff muscles. If so, start there first. If not, choose either of the strength workouts tailored to the type of surgery you had. A choice of two workouts can help keep you motivated.
- **Pick up weights correctly.** To prevent back problems, hinge from the hips and slightly bend your knees when picking up weights.
- **Hold weights firmly.** During exercises, hold weights or resistance bands firmly, but not too tightly.
- **Check posture and positioning.** Look in a mirror every now and then (see "Posture Check" in Chapter 9 and the following positioning tips) so that good form will become second nature.
  - Keep your wrists firm (straight as a pipe) as you lift and lower weights.

- Keep knees and elbows soft rather than locking your joints.
- When you are performing a wall squat, your knees should bend only 30 to 45 degrees. Don't allow your buttocks to go below knee height to avoid putting too much pressure on your knees.

- **Breathe.** Breathe normally throughout each exercise, exhaling as you exert yourself to lift, push, or pull against resistance. If you tend to hold your breath, try counting aloud to prevent this.

- **Progress slowly.** Muscles strengthen more quickly than connective ligaments and tendons, which need time to catch up to minimize the chance of injury. Slow progression is the key to success and injury prevention. If you cannot manage all 10 reps, do what you can and work on adding reps slowly.

Building Your Routine

The advice below comes from experts—women being treated for breast cancer, breast cancer survivors, and exercise professionals:

- **Set small, achievable goals.** Start with short walks on as many days of the week as you can manage and build up to longer walks. Likewise, start with one strength training session a week and add on when you can do so.

- **Embrace wellness and commit to health.** Just try the program and see how you feel. Routine helps, so try to exercise at the same time of day. Walk in the morning, for example, if this is when you have more energy. "I can't believe what a difference exercise makes in your all-around attitude," says Laurie Durgan, a busy 47-year-old mother, who credits Joy Prouty with teaching her a range of exercises to prepare for surgery and recover from it. "We are spiritual, emotional, mental, and physical beings. When one is out of whack, the rest get out of whack. Getting my physical body going has helped me in my mental and emotional states. It just makes me feel happier."

- **Connect with friends.** Four mornings a week, Joan Lawhon, a board member of Latinas for a Cure in San Antonio, Texas, and a six-year survivor, walks three miles around a local track with a very close friend with whom she can discuss anything. "It's not just good for our bodies, it's good for our souls," she says.

- **Group up.** Merry Murray Meade, a preschool teacher with children of her own, and Dara* had never met before they started rowing on the Charles River in Boston. While Dara had enjoyed small boats as a child, neither had crewed on a team before joining forces through WeCanRow, a program designed to enhance wellness and rehabilitation for breast cancer survivors, which Olympic rower Holly Metcalf launched as part of Row as One Institute (see Resources). Team members rarely skip sessions unless they're really sick, says Dara. "We take it seriously because we love it and we love being together. We have fun." Adds Meade, "Rowing has given me strength and endurance. It pushed me to know I can take on something new, which is kind of cool at my age."

- **Problem solve.** Karen Jackson is founder and CEO of Sisters Network, Inc., a national organization dedicated to promoting breast health education and supporting African American survivors and community. At 62, Ms. Jackson is very active physically, too—she rides a bike, walks, and swims. "All of these activities can be enjoyed alone if you are unable to find a partner," she notes. "If you wait for somebody to join you, you may never, ever get around to exercising. Make your exercise program a top priority." If you get derailed—whether because of exhaustion, a move, or a time crunch—try again.

- **Enjoy good days, accept bad days.** Any exercise is better than none, so it helps to do whatever you can. Terri Gray, a vibrant woman with metastatic breast cancer, slows down at

---

*Not her actual name

times when anticancer drugs prove especially taxing. On days when her energy is in short supply she gives herself permission to do little, perhaps just joining her husband in taking their three Boston terriers for a walk. "Sometimes, my walk is barely a stroll," she reports. "I'm holding onto my husband's elbow and saying, 'Pretend we're 99—that's what I feel like today!'" Otherwise, she's a dynamo, walking full speed ahead and attending Jazzercise classes several days a week.

- **Celebrate every victory.** As Gloria Wade-Lessier recovered from the first of three bouts with breast cancer, her legs were so weak that a physical therapist had her do all of her exercises in a swimming pool at her Nevada home. "It took me a long time to get stronger, but I did," she says. "I did exercises in the swimming pool. Then I could walk a little farther, a little longer." Now she goes to the gym three times a week.

- **Expand your activities.** Once you're feeling more like your old self, branch out. Yoga, Pilates, and tai chi are fine flexibility exercises; yoga and Pilates strengthen muscles, as well. Dancing, swimming, climbing stairs, running, and cycling offer cardiovascular benefits.

- **Recapture joy.** Sally Edwards, a professional athlete and author of *Heart Zones Training*, notes that the joy of motion often gets lost as girls who reveled in riding a bike, sinking a basketball, or hitting a softball grow up. "People need to do activities that they love," she says. Sometimes exercise is a vehicle to get you to the point where you can do what you love. Other times, it's an enjoyable end in itself. If you're bored, try something new! (See Resources.)

The Right Timing

Ideally, you would begin this comprehensive program before you had surgery. That way, you'd have a better sense of your usual range of motion and strength before surgery, which would help you work toward regaining these afterward. You'd also be in better physical condition overall, which could ease your journey through treatment and speed your recovery.

Most likely, though, you are somewhere along the path of treatment or recovery. If you had surgery on one breast, try comparing the range of motion and strength on that side of your body to your other side. This will give you a sense of the changes brought about by surgery that your workouts will help you address. If you had surgery on both breasts, your workouts will help you aim for a full or comfortable range of motion and improvements in strength on both sides of your body.

Before starting our program, get advice and permission from your doctor. For approximate timing of activities, which vary depending on the extent of your surgery and how swiftly your body heals, see Table 10.1.

Exercise Logs

Copy these exercise logs and use them to record your progress. Add information each time you exercise:

- **Posture.** Mark off posture checks each day.
- **Walking.** Write down the minutes or steps.
- **Balance.** Write down the balance exercises from your workout and record when you have done them.
- **Stretches.** Write down the stretches from your workout and record when you have done them.
- **Strength training.** Write down the strength exercises from your workout. On workout days, record repetitions, sets, and the amount of weight you are using for each strength exercise. This will change as you progress.

Measuring your progress motivates and encourages you to continue with your program. Referring back to your baseline assessments in Chapter 9 will help you see the changes. As you go forward, you also may notice a difference in how you feel throughout the day.

TABLE 10.1 The Right Timing

Type of Surgery	Posture Practice	Walking	Balance Exercises	Stretches*	Strength Exercises*
Lumpectomy	Right away	Right away	1 week after surgery	1 week after surgery	2 weeks after surgery
Sentinel Node Surgery	1 day after surgery	1 day after surgery	1 week after surgery	1–2 weeks after surgery	2–4 weeks after surgery
Axillary Node Surgery	1 day after surgery	1 day after surgery	1–2 weeks after surgery	2 weeks after surgery	4 weeks after surgery
Mastectomy	1 day after surgery	1 day after surgery	1–2 weeks after surgery	2 weeks after surgery	4 weeks after surgery
Implant	1 day after surgery	1 day after surgery	1–2 weeks after surgery	3–6 weeks after surgery	12 weeks after surgery
TRAM Flap	1 day after surgery	1 day after surgery	2–4 weeks after surgery	3–6 weeks after surgery	12 weeks after surgery
Lat Flap	1 day after surgery	1 day after surgery	2–4 weeks after surgery	3–6 weeks after surgery	12 weeks after surgery

*Typically, your surgical drains should be removed before you embark on stretching or strength-training exercises.

Breast Cancer Survivor's Log
Phase I: Posture Checks and Walking

Review "The Right Timing" chart (Table 10.1) with your doctor before adding start dates for posture checks and walking. Record days when you do posture checks. Also record days and time or steps for walking.

Activity	Monday	Tuesday	Wednesday	Thursday	Friday	Saturday	Sunday
Posture Checks *Start Date:*							
Walking *Start Date:* *Time or Steps:*							

Breast Cancer Survivor's Log
Phase II: Posture Checks, Walking, Balance, and Stretches

Review "The Right Timing" chart (Table 10.1, page 138) with your doctor before adding start dates for Balance and Stretches. Write in your balance and stretch exercises from the workout tailored to your surgery in Chapter 12. Record days and time or steps for walking. Also record when you do posture checks and your balance and stretch workout.

Activity	Monday	Tuesday	Wednesday	Thursday	Friday	Saturday	Sunday
Posture Checks							
Walking *Time or Steps:*							
Balance *Start Date:*							
Stretches *Start Date:*							

Breast Cancer Survivor's Log
Phase III: Strength Training

Review "The Right Timing" chart (Table 10.1, page 138) with your doctor before starting the Chapter 12 strength training workout tailored to your surgery. At each strength training session, record reps/sets/weight as shown in the example in the first box. This will change as you progress. If you're doing more than one set, start at the beginning of the workout again and go to the end. Continue doing your Phase II exercises: posture checks, walking, balance, and stretches.

Strength Exercises		Monday	Tuesday	Wednesday	Thursday	Friday	Saturday	Sunday
Example: Biceps Curl	Reps/Sets	10/1		10/1		10/1		
	Weight	3 lbs		3 lbs		3 lbs		
	Reps/Sets							
	Weight							
	Reps/Sets							
	Weight							
	Reps/Sets							
	Weight							
	Reps/Sets							
	Weight							
	Reps/Sets							
	Weight							
	Reps/Sets							
	Weight							
	Reps/Sets							
	Weight							
	Reps/Sets							
	Weight							
	Reps/Sets							
	Weight							
	Reps/Sets							
	Weight							
	Reps/Sets							
	Weight							
	Reps/Sets							
	Weight							
	Reps/Sets							
	Weight							

The Exercises

This chapter contains the exercises you will use in your workouts. It would not be safe or helpful to choose which exercises to do just by flipping through the pages. To exercise safely, see the workouts tailored to the type of surgery you had:

- Lumpectomy or mastectomy without reconstructive surgery workouts, pages 192–200
- Breast implant workouts, pages 201–209
- TRAM workouts, pages 210–218
- Lat workouts, pages 219–227
- Save Your Shoulder workouts, pages 228–231

Shoulder Pendulum

BENEFITS: Warms up the shoulder. Improves mobility and helps restore range of motion.

STARTING POSITION: Stand with one foot in front of the other and hold onto a counter or chair for balance with the arm on your unaffected side. Hinge forward from the hips and let the arm on the side where you had surgery hang loosely toward the floor with your thumb pointing forward.

INSTRUCTIONS: Begin the movement by letting your body rock forward and backward. When you rock forward, the heel of your back foot will come up off the floor. When you rock backward, the toe of your front foot will come up off the floor. Let your arm swing gently forward and back to complete one repetition. Switch arms and repeat if you had surgery on both sides.

TECHNIQUE AND TIPS

- Focus on initiating the movement from your shoulder.
- Swing slowly and with control, letting your arm relax.
- Breathe normally throughout.

REPEAT: 10 times, once or twice a day

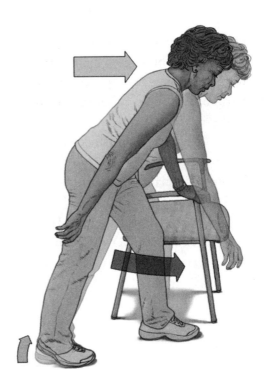

HAVING TROUBLE?

If you are uncomfortable standing, try sitting in a chair without armrests and letting your arm hang to the side to swing.

Shoulder Circles

BENEFITS: Warms up the shoulder. Improves mobility and helps restore range of motion.

STARTING POSITION: Stand with your feet comfortably apart. Hinge forward from the hips, holding onto a counter or chair for balance with the arm on your unaffected side. Let the arm on the side where you had surgery hang loosely toward the floor with your thumb pointing forward.

INSTRUCTIONS: Gently swing your arm in circles, focusing on initiating the movement from the shoulder. Reverse the direction. Switch arms and repeat if you had surgery on both sides.

TECHNIQUE AND TIPS

- Focus on initiating the swing from the shoulder.
- Swing only as much as is comfortable for your own range of motion.
- Swing slowly and with control, letting your arm relax.
- Breathe normally throughout.

REPEAT: 10 times, once or twice a day

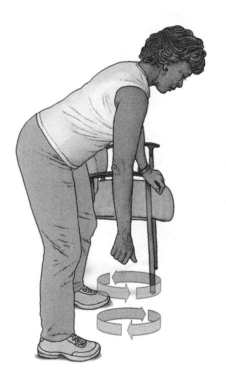

HAVING TROUBLE?

If standing is uncomfortable, try sitting near the edge of a chair without armrests. Spread your feet apart and hinge forward from the hip, resting your unaffected arm on your knee. Let your other arm hang loosely between your legs to allow it to swing in circles. Switch arms and repeat if you had surgery on both sides.

Scapula Squeezes

BENEFITS: Warms up and engages the upper and middle back and improves shoulder range of motion and mobility. Opens up the chest, which is important for good posture.

STARTING POSITION: Sit or stand with your arms at your sides.

INSTRUCTIONS: Roll your shoulders down and back away from your ears. Holding this position, squeeze your shoulder blades together and hold for 4–6 counts. Slowly return to the starting position.

TECHNIQUE AND TIPS

- As you squeeze, think of squeezing a tennis ball between your shoulder blades.
- Keep your spine in a neutral position.
- Tighten your abdominal muscles.
- Breathe normally throughout.

REPEAT: 10 times, once or twice a day

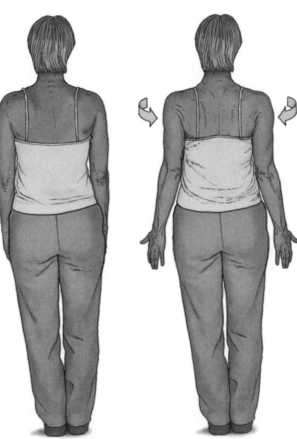

Pelvic Tilt

BENEFITS: Gently engages the abdominal muscles (rectus abdominis, internal and external obliques). This increases mobility of the lower back.

STARTING POSITION: Lie on your back with your knees bent and your feet flat on the floor approximately hip-width apart. Your spine should be in a neutral position.

INSTRUCTIONS: Tighten your abdominal muscles as you tilt your pelvis and lift your hips a bit off the floor. Slowly return to the starting position. Begin and end this exercise with a neutral spine. Tilt 3 counts, hold, release 3 counts.

TECHNIQUE AND TIPS

- You should feel as if you are pulling your hips toward your ribs and your belly button toward your spine.
- Keep your shoulders down and back away from your ears.
- Breathe normally throughout.

REPEAT: 10 times, once or twice a day

HAVING TROUBLE?

Once you recover from surgery, this will become a very easy exercise. Relax and try to pull your stomach in gently.

Heel Raises

BENEFITS: Strengthens the muscles around your ankles and the backs of your lower legs, which improves stability and enhances balance.

STARTING POSITION: Stand with feet a comfortable distance apart and weight distributed evenly on both feet.

INSTRUCTIONS: Lift your heels so you are standing on the balls of your feet. As you lift, try to hold this position and balance. Then bring your heels back down to the floor. Lift slowly, hold, then lower slowly.

TECHNIQUE AND TIPS

- In the starting position, think of your foot as a room and stand evenly on all four corners.
- When lifting up to the balls of your feet, balance evenly on the front two corners.
- Keep your ankles firm so that they don't roll outward or inward.
- Breathe normally throughout.

REPEAT: As a balance exercise 2–4 times, once or twice a day. As a strength exercise, 10 reps, 1–3 sets.

HAVING TROUBLE?

If you feel unsteady, place your hands on the back of a chair to help you balance.

Walk a Narrow Path

BENEFITS: Improves your balance. Helps restore and improve your walking gait.

STARTING POSITION: Stand evenly on both feet.

INSTRUCTIONS: Walk forward, taking 8–10 steps as if you are walking along on a narrow path. Stop, steady yourself, then walk backward. This is one complete repetition.

TECHNIQUE AND TIPS

- Focus on your posture. Your chin should be parallel to the ground.
- Look forward instead of looking down at your feet.
- Pretend you have a tray on your head.
- Relax arms at your sides and let them swing naturally forward and back.
- Breathe normally throughout.

REPEAT: 2–4 times, once or twice a day

HAVING TROUBLE?

If you feel unsteady, hold onto a wall or countertop.

Braiding

BENEFITS: Helps you transfer your weight more easily and improves your stability when moving or stepping out to the side.

STARTING POSITION: Stand with weight evenly distributed on both feet.

INSTRUCTIONS: Move toward the left side of the room to a count of 8. Lead with your left foot, cross over with your right foot, step out again with your left foot, and cross under with the right foot, step out with your left foot, cross over with your right foot, step out with your left foot, then bring your feet together and hold. When you feel steady on your feet, repeat in the opposite direction, moving toward the right side of the room. This is one complete repetition.

TECHNIQUE AND TIPS

- Focus on your posture. Your chin should be parallel to the ground.
- Look forward instead of down at your feet.
- Relax your arms at your sides.
- Breathe normally throughout.

REPEAT: 2–4 times, once or twice a day

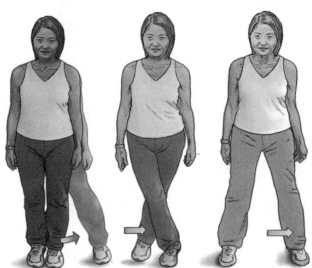

HAVING TROUBLE?

Hold onto a stable surface if you feel unsteady. If you have hip discomfort, just step out to the side and bring your feet together each time without crossing over and under.

Single Leg Stance

BENEFITS: Strengthens the hip of the standing leg and improves balance and stability.

STARTING POSITION: Stand with your weight distributed evenly on both feet.

INSTRUCTIONS: Lift one foot slightly off the floor, shifting your weight over to the supporting leg. Try to maintain your balance for 5–20 seconds before putting your foot down. Repeat on the other leg.

TECHNIQUE AND TIPS

- Find a spot straight ahead on which to focus.
- Pull your abdominal muscles in and up.
- Keep your hips even, and do not sink into the hip of the leg you are standing on.
- Breathe normally throughout.

REPEAT: 2–4 times on each leg, once or twice a day

HAVING TROUBLE?

Hold onto a stable surface for support.

Single Arm Overhead Stretch

BENEFITS: Stretches the chest muscles and the underarm area, which may be tight after surgery. Also helps you restore a full range of motion.

STARTING POSITION: Lie on your back with your knees bent and your feet flat on the floor approximately hip-width apart. Hold your affected arm just below the wrist. Both thumbs should point upward.

INSTRUCTIONS: Relax your affected arm. Allowing your other arm to do all of the work, slowly lift your affected arm up and overhead as far as possible. Stop at the point of tightness. Hold the stretch for 5–20 seconds and then return to the starting position. Perform 2–4 times and then repeat with the other arm.

TECHNIQUE AND TIPS

- Always warm up before you stretch.
- Stretch slowly and go only to the point of tightness.
- Breathe normally throughout.

REPEAT: 2–4 times on each side, once or twice a day

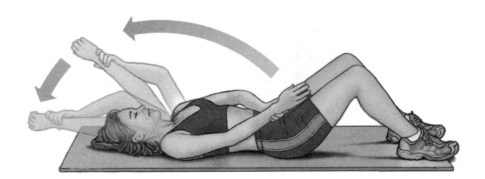

HAVING TROUBLE?

Place a pillow or two on the floor above your shoulders. As you raise the affected arm overhead, press it into the pillow.

Wall Climb: Front

BENEFITS: Stretches muscles of the chest, shoulder, and back as well as the underarm area. This improves your range of motion, which may be limited after surgery.

STARTING POSITION: Stand facing a wall. Place the hand of your affected arm on the wall at about shoulder height (or at a comfortable height if this is too difficult). Extend your affected arm as much as possible without locking the elbow. If your arm is weak and you need assistance, you may hold it near the elbow with your other hand.

INSTRUCTIONS: Walk your hand up the wall as high as you can to the point of tightness. If possible, step in toward the wall to increase the stretch with the ultimate goal of moving in right next to the wall so that you achieve full range of motion. Hold the stretch for 5–20 seconds. Slowly walk your hand back to the starting position. Perform 2–4 times and then repeat with the other arm.

TECHNIQUE AND TIPS

- Always warm up before you stretch.
- To get a sense of your normal range of motion, try the exercise with the unaffected arm first. Then repeat with the affected side.
- Stop at the point of tightness, and then try to reach a little farther each time. You should never feel any pain!
- Breathe normally throughout.

REPEAT: 2–4 times on each side, once or twice a day

HAVING TROUBLE?

Progress slowly and go only to your comfortable range of motion each time. Anything you do is better than doing nothing.

Wall Climb: Side

BENEFITS: Stretches muscles of the chest, shoulder, and back as well as the underarm area. This improves your range of motion, which may be limited after surgery.

STARTING POSITION: Stand with a wall at your side. Place the hand of your affected arm on the wall lower than shoulder height. Extend this arm as much as possible without locking the elbow.

INSTRUCTIONS: Walk your hand up the wall as high as you can to the point of tightness. If possible, step in toward the wall to increase the stretch with the ultimate goal of moving in right next to the wall so that you achieve full range of motion. Hold the stretch for 5–20 seconds. Slowly walk your hand back to the starting position. Perform 2–4 times and then repeat with the other arm.

TECHNIQUE AND TIPS

- Always warm up before you stretch.
- To get a sense of your normal range of motion, try the exercise with the unaffected arm first. Then repeat with the affected side.
- Stop at the point of tightness, and then try to reach a little farther each time. You should never feel any pain!
- Breathe normally throughout.

REPEAT: 2–4 times on each side, once or twice a day

HAVING TROUBLE?

Progress slowly and go only to your comfortable range of motion each time. Anything you do is better than doing nothing.

Butterfly Stretch

BENEFITS: Stretches the chest muscles and the underarm, which may be tight after surgery.

STARTING POSITION: Lie on your back with your knees bent approximately hip-width apart and your feet flat on the floor. Place your hands behind your head with your elbows pointing toward the ceiling.

INSTRUCTIONS: Slowly lower your elbows toward the floor, stopping at the point of tightness. Hold the stretch for 5–20 seconds. Slowly return to the starting position.

TECHNIQUE AND TIPS

- Always warm up before you stretch.
- Hold the stretch without bouncing your arms.
- Breathe normally throughout.

REPEAT: 2–4 times, once or twice a day

HAVING TROUBLE?

Try placing one or two pillows underneath each elbow. As you lower your elbows, press them gently into the pillows. If your chest and underarm feel very tight, this is a good way to start the stretch, because it safely limits your range of motion. As your range of motion improves, work toward removing the pillows.

155

Side-Lying Reach

BENEFITS: Stretches your entire side, especially the underarm area, which may feel tight after surgery.

STARTING POSITION: Lie on your side on the floor or a mat. Slightly bend your knees. Rest your head on your arm.

INSTRUCTIONS: Extend your top leg straight out with the toe pointed and lift your top arm over your head for a full side stretch. Try to align your arm with your ear. Hold the stretch 5–20 seconds. Slowly return to the starting position.

TECHNIQUE AND TIPS

- Always warm up before you stretch.
- Try to make a long straight line from the tip of your fingers to your toes as you stretch.
- Keep your shoulders and hips stacked in a straight line.
- Keep your spine in a neutral position.
- Breathe normally throughout.

REPEAT: 2–4 times on each side, once or twice a day

HAVING TROUBLE?

Place a pillow under your head for comfort. You also can place a pillow above your head to limit your range of motion as you stretch your upper arm.

Seated Side Stretch

BENEFITS: Stretches the muscles along your side and underarm, which are often very tight after surgery.

STARTING POSITION: Sit on the floor with your legs crossed and both hands on the floor at your sides.

INSTRUCTIONS: Slowly lift your right arm up and over your head as if you are reaching with your palm toward the opposite wall. Bend the elbow of your other arm as you stretch. Keep your shoulders down and back away from your ears. Hold for 4–6 counts. Slowly return to the starting position.

TECHNIQUE AND TIPS

- Always warm up before you stretch.
- As you lift your arm up and over your head, your arm should be aligned with your ear.
- Be sure to keep both buttocks firmly planted on the floor.
- Breathe normally throughout.

REPEAT: 2–4 times on each side, once or twice a day

HAVING TROUBLE?

The same stretch can be performed while you sit in a chair without armrests.

Child's Pose with a Diagonal Reach

BENEFITS: Stretches the entire side of your back from your shoulder to your hip. This also is a great stretch for the lower back.

STARTING POSITION: Position yourself on your hands and knees. Walk your hands diagonally out to the right. Place your left hand on top of your right hand. Keep your shoulders down and back away from your ears.

INSTRUCTIONS: Slowly let your buttocks drop back toward your heels. Hold the stretch for 5–20 seconds. Slowly return to the starting position. Repeat on the other side, walking your hands diagonally out to the left and placing your right hand on top of your left hand. Again, let your buttocks drop back toward your heels. Hold the stretch for 5–20 seconds. Slowly return to the starting position.

TECHNIQUE AND TIPS

- Always warm up before you stretch.
- Stretch to the point of tightness.
- Breathe normally throughout.

REPEAT: 2–4 times on each side, once or twice a day

HAVING TROUBLE?

If your knees bother you, try placing a pillow behind your knees between your thighs and calves. As you sink back, this limits your range of motion. You also can place a pillow beneath your knees to make you more comfortable.

Single Arm Wall Stretch

BENEFITS: Stretches chest muscles and the underarms, which are often tight after surgery. This helps open up your shoulder so that you can comfortably stand up straight.

STARTING POSITION: Stand in a doorway and place your hand on the edge of the frame slightly lower than shoulder level with your palm facing forward. Keep both shoulders down and back away from your ears.

INSTRUCTIONS: Slowly turn your body away from the door frame until you feel the stretch in your chest and underarm. Hold for 5–20 seconds. Slowly return to the starting position.

TECHNIQUE AND TIPS

- Always warm up before you stretch.
- Stretch only to the point of tightness.
- Breathe normally throughout.

REPEAT: 2–4 times on each side, once or twice a day.

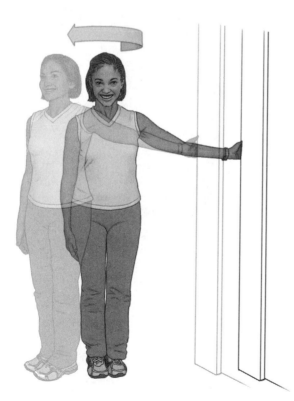

HAVING TROUBLE?

Sit with your arms in front of you at chest level and your thumbs up. Open your arms out to the side as you squeeze your shoulder blades together. Stop at the point of tightness.

Overhead Clasped Hands Stretch

BENEFITS: Stretches the muscles of your abdomen, back, shoulders, and arms. Also stretches the underarm, which may feel tight after surgery.

STARTING POSITION: Stand or sit with your feet a comfortable distance apart. Clasp your hands in front of you with your palms facing out.

INSTRUCTIONS: Slowly lift your arms up toward the ceiling only to the point of tightness. Keep your shoulders down and back away from your ears. Hold for 5–20 seconds. Slowly return to the starting position.

TECHNIQUE AND TIPS

- Always warm up before you stretch.
- Keep your chin parallel to the floor.
- As you are lifting your arms, keep your shoulders relaxed—not hunched—so they stay down and back, away from your ears.
- Breathe normally throughout.

REPEAT: 2–4 times, once or twice a day

HAVING TROUBLE?

Perform this same stretch lying on your back. If you find it uncomfortable to clasp your hands you can hold a towel at thigh level with your palms facing the floor and lift the towel upward over your head. To limit the range of motion, you may place one or two pillows above your head. As the stretch becomes easier, remove the pillows one at a time.

Chest Stretch

BENEFITS: Opens the chest and rotates the shoulders back, which is very helpful because breast surgery can cause tightness in the chest and rounded shoulders. This may cause poor posture and decreased range of motion.

STARTING POSITION: Sit or stand comfortably. Roll your shoulders down and back away from your ears, then clasp your hands behind your back.

INSTRUCTIONS: Slowly lift your hands behind you. Hold the stretch for 5–20 seconds.

TECHNIQUE AND TIPS

- Always warm up before you stretch.
- Stretch only to the point of tightness.
- Listen to your body and stop when you feel the stretch.
- Hold the stretch without bouncing.
- Breathe normally throughout.

REPEAT: 2–4 times, once or twice a day

HAVING TROUBLE?

Lie on your back with your knees bent and your feet flat on the floor and approximately hip-width apart. Open your arms out to the side on the floor to about chest level with your palms facing the ceiling. Hold for 5–20 seconds.

Shoulder Stretch

BENEFITS: Stretches your shoulder and back muscles.

STARTING POSITION: Stand or sit with your feet comfortably apart. Bring your left arm across your chest and place that hand on your right shoulder. Cup your left elbow with your right hand.

INSTRUCTIONS: Roll your shoulders down and back away from your ears. Gently pull your elbow across your chest. Stretch only to the point of tightness. Hold the stretch 5–20 seconds. Slowly return to the starting position.

TECHNIQUE AND TIPS

- Always warm up before you stretch.
- Keep your shoulders down and back away from your ear as you stretch.
- Breathe normally.

REPEAT: 2–4 times on each side, once or twice a day

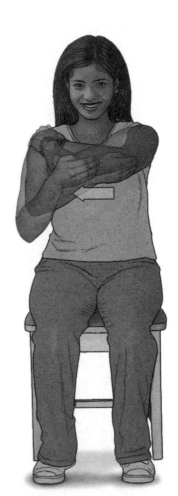

HAVING TROUBLE?

Perform this exercise while lying down on your back. You also can hold a towel at chest level in your right hand and use your left hand to pull the towel across your chest to the point of tightness.

Supine Stretch

BENEFITS: Stretches muscles that attach the hip to the torso. Eases tightness, particularly after TRAM surgery, and helps you regain comfortable, upright posture.

STARTING POSITION: Lie on your back with your knees bent and your feet flat on the floor approximately hip-width apart. Place your arms at your sides.

INSTRUCTIONS: First, focus on stretching one leg at a time. Slowly extend the leg out straight so that you are pressing your calf into the floor. Hold for 5–20 seconds. Slowly return to the starting position. Repeat with the opposite leg. When you can comfortably extend each leg, switch to extending both legs at one time.

TECHNIQUE AND TIPS

- Always warm up before you stretch.
- Move slowly and with control.
- Stretch only to the point of tightness.
- Breathe normally throughout.

REPEAT: 2–4 times, once or twice a day

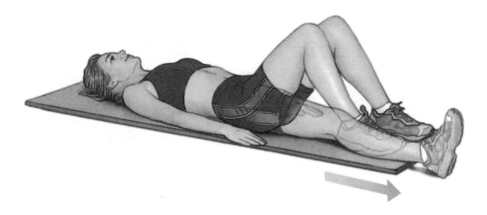

HAVING TROUBLE?

Progress slowly and go only to your comfortable range of motion each time. Anything you do is better than doing nothing.

Full Body Stretch

BENEFITS: Stretches the entire body from the tips of your fingers to the tips of your toes. This helps relax tightness in the shoulder, underarm, abdomen, and hip after surgery that may prevent you from comfortably standing up straight.

STARTING POSITION: Lie on your back with your arms relaxed at your sides. Bend your knees and place your feet flat on the floor approximately hip-width apart.

INSTRUCTIONS: Slide your legs forward until they extend as far as is comfortable. Then slowly lift and extend your arms overhead, lowering them until your hands touch the floor. Keep your elbows soft throughout the movement. Hold the stretch for 5–20 seconds. Slowly return to the starting position.

TECHNIQUE AND TIPS

- Always warm up before you stretch.
- Stretch only to the point of tightness.
- Try to make a long, straight line from fingers to toes.
- Breathe normally throughout.

REPEAT: 2–4 times, once or twice a day

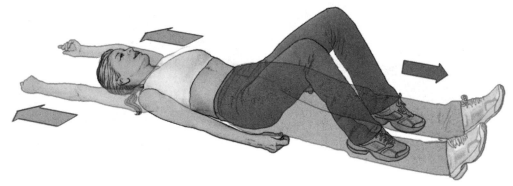

HAVING TROUBLE?

Place one or two pillows above your head to support your arms and limit your range of motion. Press your arms into the pillow as you stretch. Work toward removing the pillows as your range of motion improves.

Cat-Camel

BENEFITS: Stretches the muscles of your torso. Improves flexibility and movement from your shoulders to your hips.

STARTING POSITION: Position yourself on your hands and knees. Your spine should be in a neutral position.

INSTRUCTIONS: Rounding your upper back toward the ceiling, draw your belly button in toward your spine. Relax your head and neck and let your chin come forward toward your chest. As you release the move, lift your head and relax your back to its natural arch. Round upward 3 counts, hold, relax back down 3 counts.

TECHNIQUE AND TIPS

- Always warm up before you stretch.
- Focus on moving smoothly and naturally, rather than pushing hard at either end of the movement.
- Press your shoulders down and back away from your ears.
- Breathe normally throughout.

REPEAT: 2–4 times, once or twice a day

HAVING TROUBLE?

If kneeling is uncomfortable, place a pillow or extra mat under your knees. Also if this exercise bothers your wrists, try placing a folded towel or mat under the heels of your hands.

Kneeling Spinal Rotation

BENEFITS: Stretches the muscles of the underarm, chest, side, and back, which helps relieve tightness after surgery that can contribute to poor posture.

STARTING POSITION: Position yourself on your hands and knees on the floor or a mat. Starting with your tighter side, place that hand gently behind your head.

INSTRUCTIONS: Slowly bring the elbow down toward the floor until it is slightly behind the hand on the floor. Then slowly lift and rotate toward the ceiling. Throughout the stretch, follow your elbow with your eyes. Rotate down 3 counts, hold, rotate up 3 counts.

TECHNIQUE AND TIPS

- Always warm up before you stretch.
- Stretch only to the point of tightness.
- Notice how your range of motion increases with each repetition.
- Breathe normally throughout.

REPEAT: 2–4 times on each side, once or twice a day

HAVING TROUBLE?

Sit in a chair with your hands on your thighs. Slowly rotate your head and torso to the right. As you do so, bring your left hand across and place it on the outside of your right knee. Maintain good posture throughout the movement. Hold the stretch for 5–20 seconds. Slowly return to the starting position.

Supine Torso Rotation

BENEFITS: Stretches the muscles of your core, chest, and front of the shoulders. This helps you improve range of motion in your arms and torso, which may feel tight after surgery.

STARTING POSITION: Lie on your back with your knees bent and your feet together and flat on the floor. Place your arms comfortably out to each side just below shoulder level, palms up.

INSTRUCTIONS: Gently pull in your stomach and then lower both knees together toward one side of the floor. Keep both shoulders flat on the floor so that you feel a stretch across your chest at the same time. Hold for 5–20 seconds. Slowly bring your legs back toward the center, and then lower them to the other side. Hold again for 5–20 seconds. Slowly return to the starting position. This is one complete repetition.

TECHNIQUE AND TIPS

- Always warm up before you stretch.
- Stretch only to the point of tightness.
- Keep your shoulders relaxed and pressing into the floor.
- Breathe normally throughout.

REPEAT: 2–4 times, once or twice a day

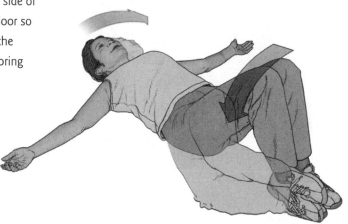

HAVING TROUBLE?

Instead of starting with your feet together, try starting with your knees bent and your feet flat on the floor approximately hip-width apart. Slowly lower your knees toward the floor, going only to your comfortable range of motion each time. Anything you do is better than doing nothing.

Prone Press Up

BENEFITS: Stretches abdominal muscles, which are often tight after surgery, and strengthens muscles that run along the spine (spinal extensors).

STARTING POSITION: Lie on your stomach on the floor or on a mat. Place your hands next to your shoulders with your palms down.

INSTRUCTIONS: Slowly press upward, lifting your head, shoulders, and chest off of the floor. As you press up, try to extend your arms as much as is comfortable. Lift 3 counts, hold, lower 3 counts.

TECHNIQUE AND TIPS

- Always warm up before you stretch.
- Lift only to the point of tightness. You should feel no pain in your lower back.
- Breathe normally, exhaling as you lift.

REPEAT: 2–4 times, once or twice a day

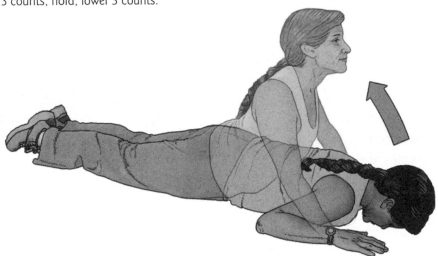

HAVING TROUBLE?

Keep your elbows on the floor while pressing upward. Another option is to stand and place your hands on your lower back with your fingertips pointing downward to the floor and then point your elbows toward the back wall. Stay within a comfortable range of motion.

Kneeling Hip Flexor Stretch

BENEFITS: Stretches muscles at the front of the hips. These muscles may become very tight after surgery, which can prevent you from comfortably standing up straight.

STARTING POSITION: Kneel on the floor or on a mat.

INSTRUCTIONS: Place your left foot out in front of you with your knee aligned directly above your ankle. Keep your hips squared. Place your hands on your left thigh just above your knee. Slowly press forward until you feel the stretch in the front of your right hip. Hold the stretch for 5–20 seconds. Slowly return to the starting position.

TECHNIQUE AND TIPS

- Always warm up before you stretch.
- Keep your abdominal muscles pulled in and your torso upright, maintaining a neutral spine.
- Stretch only to the point of tightness.
- Do not bounce.
- Breathe normally throughout.

REPEAT: 2–4 times on each side, once or twice a day

HAVING TROUBLE?

Lie on your back with both legs extended. Pull one knee in toward your chest, holding that leg at the back of the thigh. Flex the foot of the extended leg and press your calf into the floor. You should feel the stretch in front of the hip of the extended leg. Repeat on the other side. If the muscles at the front of your hips are very tight, you may want to start by holding the stretch for 5 seconds and then gradually work up to 20 seconds.

Supine Hip Flexor Stretch

BENEFITS: Stretches muscles that attach hip to trunk. Eases tightness after surgery and helps you regain comfortable, upright posture.

STARTING POSITION: Lie on your back on the floor or a mat. Hold one leg behind the thigh with your knee pulled toward your chest. Extend your other leg straight along the floor.

INSTRUCTIONS: Flex the foot of the leg on the floor so that the toes point toward the ceiling as you press the calf down toward the floor. At the same time, draw the knee of your other leg as close to your chest as is comfortable. You should feel the stretch in front of your extended leg. Hold the stretch for 5–20 seconds. Slowly return to the starting position.

TECHNIQUE AND TIPS

- Always warm up before you stretch.
- Stretch only to the point of tightness.
- Breathe normally throughout.

REPEAT: 2–4 times with each leg, once or twice a day.

HAVING TROUBLE?

Lie on a bed close to one side of it. Bend the knee of the inside leg and place that foot flat on the bed. Drop your outside leg off the side of the bed until you feel the stretch in front of that hip and thigh.

Supine Hamstring Stretch

BENEFITS: Stretches the muscles at the back of the upper leg. This helps correct imbalances after surgery that can lead to poor posture.

STARTING POSITION: Lie on your back with both legs extended. Lift one leg, holding it behind your thigh so that your knee is directly above your hip.

INSTRUCTIONS: Flex your foot and lift your heel toward the ceiling, straightening your leg as much as possible without locking the knee. Hold the stretch for 5–20 seconds. Slowly return to the starting position.

TECHNIQUE AND TIPS

- Always warm up before you stretch.
- Relax your shoulders and upper back into the floor.
- Extend your leg only to the point of mild tightness, being careful to avoid feeling pressure behind your knee.
- Breathe normally, exhaling as you extend and stretch the leg.

REPEAT: 2–4 times with each leg, once or twice a day

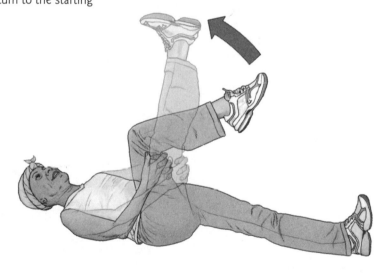

HAVING TROUBLE?

If it is difficult for you to hold your leg as you extend it, you can use a towel, bathrobe tie, or stretch strap to assist you. Another option is to bend the knee of the leg that is on the floor.

Standing Internal Shoulder Rotation

BENEFITS: Strengthens a rotator cuff muscle (subscapularis) that is often weakened by surgery. This will help you regain strength and mobility in the shoulder.

STARTING POSITION: Place a small towel under your arm, just above your elbow. Hold a resistance tube or band that is knotted securely around a doorknob. Stand comfortably with your elbow at your side near your waist and your hand extended out to the side like an open door.

INSTRUCTIONS: Keep your body still and your wrist firm while slowly rotating your arm so that your hand comes across your body at waist level. Slowly return to the starting position. Rotate inward 3 counts, hold, then rotate outward 3 counts, keeping the movement slow and controlled.

TECHNIQUE AND TIPS

- Keep your wrist in a neutral position so that there is a straight line from elbow to knuckles.
- Keep your shoulders down and back away from your ears.
- To ensure that your shoulder does the work, it is very important to hold your body still throughout the movement.
- Breathe normally throughout.

REPS: 10 with each arm   **SETS:** 1–3

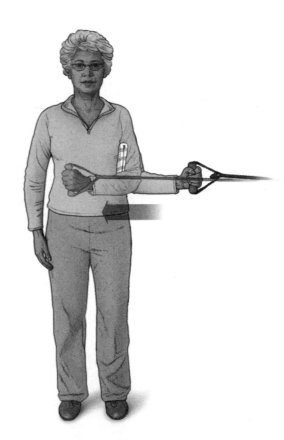

HAVING TROUBLE?

Use the lightest resistance tube or band available. Another option is to do the exercise without any equipment, just moving through the range of motion. As you improve, try adding light resistance. You also can perform this exercise while seated in a chair without armrests.

Standing External Shoulder Rotation

BENEFITS: Strengthens muscles of the rotator cuff (infraspinatus, teres minor), which are often weakened by surgery so that the shoulder rolls forward. This improves posture and helps you regain strength and mobility in the shoulder.

STARTING POSITION: Place a small towel under your arm, just above your elbow. Hold a resistance tube or band that is knotted securely around a doorknob. Stand comfortably with your elbow at your side and your forearm lying against the front of your waist.

INSTRUCTIONS: Keep your body still and your wrist firm while you slowly rotate your arm outward. Your arm should stay at waist level throughout the move. Slowly return to the starting position. Rotate outward 3 counts, hold, then rotate inward 3 counts, keeping the movement slow and controlled.

TECHNIQUE AND TIPS

- Keep your wrist in a neutral position so that there is a straight line from elbow to knuckles.
- Keep your elbow close to your body throughout the exercise as if it is the hinge on a door.
- To ensure that your shoulder does the work, it is very important to hold your body still throughout the movement.
- Breathe normally throughout.

REPS: 10 with each arm   **SETS:** 1–3

HAVING TROUBLE?

Use the lightest resistance tube or band available. Another option is to do the exercise without any equipment, just moving through the range of motion. As you improve try adding light resistance. You also can perform this exercise while seated in a chair without armrests.

173

Side-Lying External Shoulder Rotation

BENEFITS: Strengthens muscles of the rotator cuff (infraspinatus, teres minor). After surgery, tightness in the chest may pull your shoulder forward. This exercise helps you strengthen your shoulder and improves your posture.

STARTING POSITION: Lie on your side with your head resting on your arm or a pillow. Bend your knees slightly. Place a towel under your top (outer) arm between your underarm and elbow. Holding a weight in this hand, bend your arm so that your elbow is close to your waist.

INSTRUCTIONS: Initiating the movement from your shoulder, slowly lift the weight toward the ceiling. Think of your upper arm from your shoulder to your elbow as the hinge on a door. Slowly return to the starting position. Lift 3 counts, hold, lower 3 counts, keeping the movement slow and controlled.

TECHNIQUE AND TIPS

- Keep your elbow still and close to your ribs.
- Keep your wrist neutral and firm throughout the movement.
- Breathe normally, exhaling as you lift.

REPS: 10 with each arm   **SETS:** 1–3

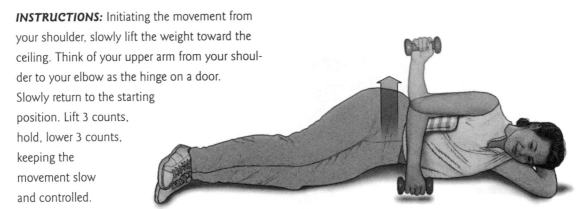

HAVING TROUBLE?

Do the exercise without any weight. Limit your range of motion, increasing it gradually as you are able to do so.

Biceps Curl

BENEFITS: Strengthens the front upper arm muscles (biceps). This helps stabilize the shoulder joint and gives you strength when lifting.

STARTING POSITION: Stand holding the weights at your sides with a firm wrist and your thumbs facing forward.

INSTRUCTIONS: Slowly bend your elbows, bringing the weights up with your palms facing your shoulders. Your thumbs will rotate outward slightly to do so. Your elbows should stay close to your ribs. Slowly lower the weights down to the starting position. Lift 3 counts, hold, down 3 counts.

TECHNIQUE AND TIPS

- Roll your shoulders down and back away from your ears. To maintain alignment, think of squeezing a tennis ball between your shoulder blades.
- Keep your shoulders still throughout the movement.
- Keep your wrists firm in a neutral position and your fingers relaxed rather than gripping the weights hard.
- Soften your knees slightly to maintain neutral posture.
- Breathe normally, exhaling as you lift.

REPS: 10   **SETS:** 1–3

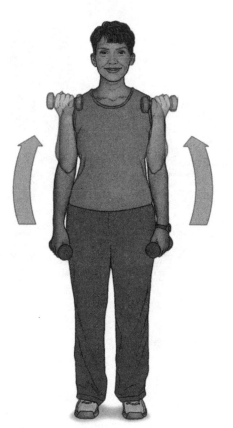

HAVING TROUBLE?

Perform the exercise with a lighter weight until you are ready to progress. If maintaining proper posture or control is still difficult, try curling one arm at a time. Lifting one or both weights while seated in a chair without armrests makes the exercise easier, too.

Seated Row

BENEFITS: Strengthens muscles of the back (latissimus dorsi, rhomboids, middle trapezius), upper front arm (biceps), and back of the shoulder (posterior deltoids). These are the muscles that help you stand up straight.

STARTING POSITION: Sit up straight on a chair, holding the handles of a resistance tube or band in both hands. Your thumbs are facing up. The band should be securely knotted around a doorknob or wrapped around a pole or banister slightly below the level of your chest. Another option is to use a tube or band with a special door attachment.

INSTRUCTIONS: While holding the resistance tube or band straight out in front of you, squeeze your shoulder blades together. Slowly bend your arms and draw your elbows back, keeping them close to your sides as you pull your fists toward your ribs. Slowly return to the starting position. Pull back 3 counts, hold, release 3 counts.

TECHNIQUE AND TIPS

- Keep your spine in a neutral position.
- Keep your abdominal muscles firm and your shoulders down and back away from your ears.
- Keep your wrists firm and straight like a pipe when holding the tube or band.
- Breathe normally, exhaling as you pull back.

REPS: 10   **SETS:** 1–3

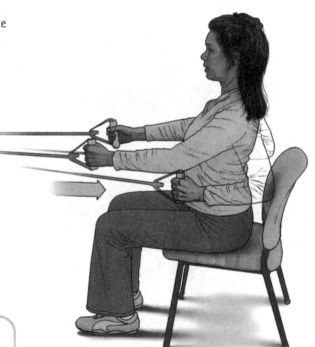

HAVING TROUBLE?

Begin with the lightest resistance tube or band available, or perform the move without any equipment at all. Another option is to do the exercise with one arm at a time.

Bent Over Row

BENEFITS: Strengthens muscles of the back (latissimus dorsi, rhomboids, trapezius), back of the shoulders (posterior deltoids), and the front of the upper arm (biceps). All help you improve your posture and stand up straight.

STARTING POSITION: Kneel on a bench or chair with your left knee and put your right foot on the floor. Hinge forward from your hips and place your left hand directly under your shoulder on the chair. Hold the weight with your right hand hanging straight down from the shoulder. Your spine should be in a neutral position and your shoulders and hips should be squared.

INSTRUCTIONS: Slightly squeeze your shoulder blades together. Slowly lift the weight close to your side, bringing it toward your ribs. Slowly return to the starting position. Lift 3 counts, hold, lower 3 counts.

TECHNIQUE AND TIPS

- Keep your abdominal muscles firm.
- As you lower the weight, avoid locking your elbows.
- Breathe normally, exhaling as you lift.

REPS: 10 on each side   **SETS:** 1–3

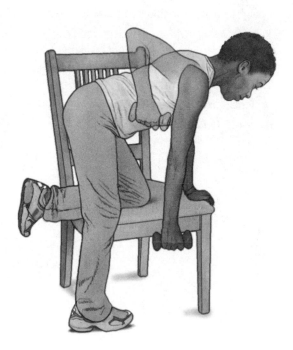

HAVING TROUBLE?

Try using a lighter weight or perform the movement without a weight.

Triceps Extension

BENEFITS: Strengthens muscles in the back of the upper arm (triceps). This helps you extend your arms, for example when pushing up out of a chair or bathtub or lowering an object.

STARTING POSITION: Lie on your back with your knees bent and your feet flat on the floor approximately hip-width apart. Holding a weight at each of its ends, extend your arms toward the ceiling. Your arms should be extended directly above your shoulders with thumbs pointing back. Keep a straight line from shoulder to elbow to wrist to knuckles.

INSTRUCTIONS: Slowly bend at the elbow and lower the weight toward the spot where your hair meets your forehead. Lower 3 counts, hold, lift 3 counts.

TECHNIQUE AND TIPS

- Keep your shoulders down and back away from your ears by gently pressing both shoulders into the floor.
- As you lower the weight toward your forehead, keep your elbows pointing toward the ceiling.
- Keep your wrists in a neutral position and do not squeeze the weight too tightly.
- Breathe normally, exhaling as you lift.

REPS: 10   **SETS:** 1–3

HAVING TROUBLE?

Perform the exercise with a lighter weight or without using any weight until you are ready to progress.

Pull Over

BENEFITS: Strengthens several back muscles (latissimus dorsi, teres minor, serratus anterior), chest muscles (pectoralis major), and muscles at the back of the upper arm (triceps). If one or both latissimus muscles have been used for reconstruction, this exercise is especially important because it recruits and strengthens surrounding muscles.

STARTING POSITION: Lie on your back with your knees bent and your feet flat on the floor approximately hip-width apart. Wrap both hands around the center bar of a single weight with your thumbs pointing back. Extend your arms straight up over your chest, while keeping your shoulders down on the floor and your elbows slightly soft, rather than locked. Your wrists should be in a firm, neutral position.

INSTRUCTIONS: Slowly lower the weight over your head toward the floor until your biceps (front of upper arms) are in line with your ears. Pull in your abdominal muscles and slowly lift the weight back to the starting position. Lower 3 counts, hold, lift 3 counts.

TECHNIQUE AND TIPS

- Keep your wrists, neck, and spine in a neutral position throughout the movement, especially when your arms are above your head.
- Before you begin the move, squeeze your shoulder blades down and back to stabilize your shoulders.
- As you lift the weight upward to return to the starting position, press your upper back gently into the floor or mat.
- Move in a slow, controlled manner.
- Breathe normally, exhaling as you lift.

REPS: 10   **SETS:** 1–3

HAVING TROUBLE?

If your shoulders and underarms feel extremely tight, place a pillow behind your head to limit your range of motion. You also may perform the exercise without weights and then slowly progress to a light weight.

Back Fly

BENEFITS: Strengthens muscles on your upper back and the back of your shoulder (trapezius, rhomboids, and posterior deltoids). A key exercise for increasing stability and strengthening the upper back, which will help you regain proper posture.

STARTING POSITION: Sit comfortably on a chair with no armrests. Hold your hand weights at your sides with your palms facing toward your body and your thumbs forward. Hinge your torso forward from the hips toward your knees while keeping your head and spine in a neutral position.

INSTRUCTIONS: Squeeze your shoulder blades together. Slowly lift the weights out to the sides until your arms are about shoulder height. Keep your elbows soft. Your palms are now facing the floor with your thumbs facing forward. Slowly lower the weights to the starting position. Lift 3 counts, hold, down 3 counts.

TECHNIQUE AND TIPS

- Try to initiate the move by squeezing your shoulder blades together as if you are squeezing a tennis ball between them and then lift the weights.
- Put your brain in the middle of the muscle group you are working. Focusing your thoughts this way helps you work muscles more efficiently.
- Breathe normally, exhaling as you lift.

REPS: 10   **SETS:** 1–3

HAVING TROUBLE?

Try this exercise without any weight. Another option is to alternate your arms, performing this exercise as a single lift on one arm at a time.

V Raise

BENEFITS: Strengthens muscles in the front and middle of the shoulder (anterior deltoid, medial deltoid). This exercise stabilizes the shoulder joint and builds up muscles that allow you to lift your arms, which can be weakened by surgery.

STARTING POSITION: Stand with weights at your side and thumbs pointing forward. Lift your chest and roll your shoulders down and back away from your ears.

INSTRUCTIONS: Slowly extend your arms in a V as you raise your weights. Keep your thumbs up throughout the movement and lift no higher than your shoulders. Slowly return to the starting position. Lift 3 counts, hold, lower 3 counts.

TECHNIQUE AND TIPS

- Squeeze your shoulder blades together before you raise the weights.
- Throughout the movement, keep your elbows soft, rather than locked, and your knees relaxed to help maintain neutral posture.
- Keep your shoulders down and back away from your ears.
- Keep your wrists firm and your fingers relaxed.
- Breathe normally, exhaling as you lift.

REPS: 10   **SETS:** 1–3

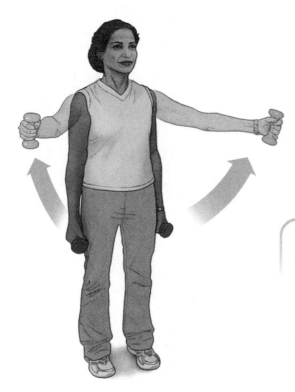

HAVING TROUBLE?

Perform the exercise with a lighter weight or without using any weight at all until you are ready to progress. Or try alternating arms as you do the movement instead of lifting both arms at once. You also can perform the exercise while seated in a chair without armrests.

Wall Push-Up

BENEFITS: Strengthens muscles of the chest (pectoralis major, pectoralis minor), front of the shoulder (anterior deltoids), and the back of the upper arm (triceps). These muscles are often weak after surgery.

STARTING POSITION: Stand facing a wall with your feet together or slightly apart. Extend your arms straight without locking your elbows and place your hands on the wall with your fingertips at shoulder level.

INSTRUCTIONS: Tighten your abdominal muscles. Slowly lower your chest toward the wall, keeping your elbows close to your ribs. Slowly return to the starting position. Lower 3 counts, hold, lift 3 counts.

TECHNIQUE AND TIPS

- Keep your shoulders down and back away from your ears.
- Keep your neck and spine in a neutral position.
- Keep your body in a straight line from head to heels.
- Breathe normally, exhaling as you push away from the wall.

REPS: 10   **SETS:** 1–3

HAVING TROUBLE?

Limit your range of motion by lowering yourself only as much as you can while maintaining proper form.

Quadruped Transverse Abdominis

BENEFITS: Strengthens muscles supporting the lower abdomen (transversus abdominis). This will help keep your core strong and stabilize your spine, which is especially important if you had a TRAM reconstruction.

STARTING POSITION: Position yourself on your hands and knees on the floor or on a mat.

INSTRUCTIONS: Keep your head in line with your spine and maintain this neutral position through-out the exercise. Without moving your spine at all, pull your abdominal muscles in as much as you can. Hold for 4–6 counts, then slowly release.

TECHNIQUE AND TIPS

- Think of pulling your belly button toward your spine.
- This is a small movement that only requires pulling in your abdominal muscles. The key is to keep your back totally still throughout the exercise.
- Keep your shoulders and hips squared.
- Breathe normally throughout.

REPS: 10   **SETS:** 1–3

HAVING TROUBLE?

Lie down on your stomach with your hands by your shoulders and your elbows resting on the floor. Pull in your abdominal muscles, lifting your belly button slightly off the floor. Hold for 4–6 counts, then release.

Opposite Arm and Leg Raise

BENEFITS: Strengthens your back, which is often weakened due to poor posture or reconstructive surgery. Works the muscles that run along your spine (spinal extensors) and muscles of the buttocks (gluteus maximus), upper back of your legs (hamstrings), and shoulder (deltoids).

STARTING POSITION: Kneel on all fours with your hands and knees directly aligned under your shoulders and hips. Keep your head and spine in a neutral position.

INSTRUCTIONS: Slowly extend your right leg off the floor behind you. At the same time, reach out in front of you with your left arm. Try to get your arm and opposite leg parallel to the floor. Slowly return to the starting position. Lift 3 counts, hold, down 3 counts. Repeat on the other side. This is one complete repetition.

TECHNIQUE AND TIPS

- Keep your head still.
- Maintain proper alignment by keeping your shoulders and hips squared.
- Imagine that while you are lengthening your torso, someone is pulling your arm and leg in opposite directions.
- If we placed a little bottle of water along the small of your back, it should not fall off. Try it!
- Breathe normally throughout.

REPS: 10   **SETS:** 1–3

HAVING TROUBLE?

Start off by lifting just your right arm and then your left arm, or your right leg and then your left leg. When you feel comfortable, proceed to simultaneously lifting the opposite arm and leg.

Oblique Press with Hand on Knee

BENEFITS: Strengthens the abdominal muscles (rectus abdominis, internal and external obliques) without straining the head or neck and helps create support for your core.

STARTING POSITION: Lie on your back with both of your knees bent and your feet flat on the floor. Keeping the knee bent, lift your right leg up. Reach across with your left arm and place the palm of your left hand on your thigh below your right knee.

INSTRUCTIONS: Press your palm against your thigh. At the same time, press your thigh against your palm to create opposition. Hold this position for 4–6 counts and then release it. Perform the press 10 times. Repeat on your opposite side using your right hand and left thigh.

TECHNIQUE AND TIPS

- To avoid holding your breath, count out loud.
- Keep your head and shoulders on the floor or mat throughout the exercise.
- Breathe normally throughout.

REPS: 10 on each side   **SETS:** 1–3

HAVING TROUBLE?

Do a pelvic tilt instead (page 147), holding for 4–6 counts and then releasing. Do this 10 times.

Crunch with Leg Extended and Rotation

BENEFITS: Adding rotation to a crunch strengthens the side (internal and external obliques) and central (rectus abdominis) abdominal muscles that work like a corset to support your core. These muscles help you bend at your waist and rotate your spine.

STARTING POSITION: Lie on your back. Bend your right knee and put that foot flat on the floor. Extend your left leg straight out on the floor. Place your right hand gently behind your head for support. Place your left hand on your right thigh.

INSTRUCTIONS: Start the move by pulling in your belly and pressing your ribs down toward your hips. As you slowly lift and rotate your body to the right, slide your left hand toward the outer edge of your bent knee. Keep your neck in neutral position so that your head is aligned with your torso. Slowly return to the starting position. Lift 3 counts, hold, down 3 counts. Perform 10 crunches. Repeat with your left knee bent and your right leg extended.

TECHNIQUE AND TIPS

- Be sure to make your abdominal muscles do the lifting rather than your head and neck. Engage your abdominal muscles before initiating the lift by pressing your ribs toward your hips and pulling your belly button in.
- Breathe normally, exhaling as you lift.

REPS: 10 on each side   **SETS:** 1–3

HAVING TROUBLE?

Make your range of motion smaller by lifting up only slightly.

Reverse Curl with Ball

BENEFITS: Strengthens key abdominal muscles (rectus abdominis, internal and external obliques), which improves core stability.

STARTING POSITION: Lie on your back and place your legs over the ball. Place your arms at your sides on the floor with your palms down.

INSTRUCTIONS: Pull your belly button toward your spine while tilting your pelvis. Use your abdominal muscles to lift the ball slowly off the floor by bringing your hips towards your rib cage. Hold and then slowly return to starting position. Lift 3 counts, hold, down 3 counts.

TECHNIQUE AND TIPS

- Be sure to move slowly and with control, rather than letting momentum do the work.
- Keep your shoulders down and touching the floor.
- Focus on having your abdominal muscles do the work, not your arms.
- Breathe normally, exhaling as you lift.

REPS: 10   **SETS:** 1–3

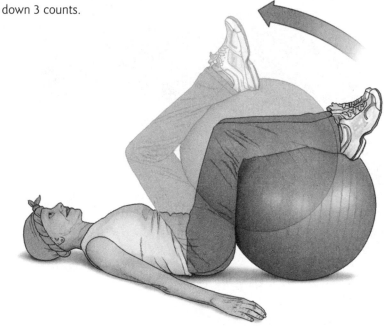

HAVING TROUBLE?

Deflate the ball slightly so it is easier to grab with your legs.

Modified Side Bridge

BENEFITS: Strengthens the muscles that stabilize your spine (quadratus lumborum, transversus abdominis, and internal and external obliques) without putting too much pressure onto the disks. This helps build a strong core.

STARTING POSITION: Lie on your right side with your hands crossed over your chest. Your shoulders and hips should be aligned. Place a rolled pillow under your neck so that you can maintain a neutral spine.

INSTRUCTIONS: Tighten your abdominal muscles. Try to raise both legs together slightly off the floor while your head stays on the pillow. If your head lifts off the pillow a bit it is important to keep your neck in a neutral position with your head, neck, and spine all aligned. Lift and hold your legs for 4–6 counts before slowly returning to the starting position. Perform the modified side bridge 10 times. Repeat on your left side.

TECHNIQUE AND TIPS

- Keep your head and spine in a neutral position.
- Keep your shoulders down and back away from your ears.
- Breathe normally, exhaling as you lift.

REPS: 10 on each side   **SETS:** 1–3

HAVING TROUBLE?

To further improve your balance, place the hand of your upper arm on the floor. Your elbow will be at a right angle and your hand will be by your waist. Now try the exercise again. If you are still having trouble, try lifting just your top leg instead of lifting both legs. If this exercise bothers your hip, perform it on a mat.

Bridge

BENEFITS: Bridges strengthen the muscles of the buttocks (gluteus maximus) and the back of the upper leg (hamstrings). This exercise also helps build core strength by promoting hip and torso stability.

STARTING POSITION: Lie on your back with your knees bent and your feet flat on the floor about hip-width apart. Place your arms on the floor at your sides with your palms facing upward to open up the shoulder joints.

INSTRUCTIONS: Squeeze your buttocks and lift your hips up off the floor only as high as you comfortably can. Lift 3 counts, hold, down 3 counts.

TECHNIQUE AND TIPS

- Keep your knees aligned over your feet.
- Keep your hips even as you lift upward.
- Keep your spine in a neutral position, rather than arching it.
- Breathe normally throughout.

REPS: 10   **SETS:** 1–3

HAVING TROUBLE?

Be sure to squeeze your buttocks before lifting your hips. This helps prevent cramping in the hamstring muscles at the back of your upper legs. You also can place a small ball or pillow between your knees to help keep your knees aligned over your feet.

Wall Squats

BENEFITS: Strengthens your legs by working muscles of the thighs (quadriceps), back of the upper legs (hamstrings), and the buttocks (gluteals).

STARTING POSITION: Stand with your back to a wall. If you have a stability ball, place it in the middle of your back at your beltline with your feet hip-width apart. Walk your feet out about 18 inches to 2 feet. Keep your shoulders down and back away from your ears. If you are not using a stability ball, your shoulders always should be in contact with the wall.

INSTRUCTIONS: Leaning back into the wall, slowly bend your knees and slide down the wall or ball, keeping your hips, knees, and feet pointing straight ahead. Lower yourself to the point where your knees are directly in line above your ankles (30 to 45 degrees). Do not go farther. Never let your hips go below the level of your knees. Slowly return to the starting position. Down 3 counts, hold, up 3 counts.

TECHNIQUE AND TIPS

- Keep your chest lifted and your chin parallel to the ground.
- As you lower yourself, think of sitting in a chair.
- To protect your knees, only go down as far as feels comfortable.
- Focus on your knees tracking toward your second toe.
- Move in a slow, controlled manner and breathe normally, exhaling as you lift up.

REPS: 10   **SETS:** 1–3

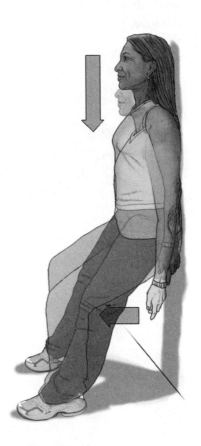

HAVING TROUBLE?

If your knees bother you, make your squats smaller. You can place a small ball between your knees to keep them aligned. Another option is to try stand-ups. Sitting in a chair, stand up and then sit back down with or without assistance from your hands.

CHAPTER 12

The Workouts

- Talk to your doctor about timing before you start any workouts.
- If you had a mastectomy or traditional lymph node surgery, please review the "Save Your Shoulder" sidebar in Chapter 9, page 109, and begin with the Save Your Shoulder Workouts, page 228.
- Remember, quality is more important than quantity. If you cannot do all the repetitions, do fewer at first and add on gradually as you progress. Focus on good form, move slowly, and remain in control throughout each move. If doing more than one set, repeat the exercises from the beginning.

This workout is for women who had a lumpectomy or mastectomy without reconstruction.

1. Shoulder Pendulum
page 144

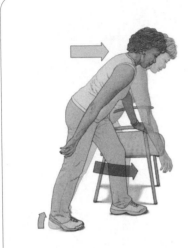

REPEAT: 10 times, once or twice a day

2. Wall Climb: Side
page 154

REPEAT: 2–4 times on each side, once or twice a day

3. Single Arm Overhead Stretch
page 152

REPEAT: 2–4 times on each side, once or twice a day

4. Supine Torso Rotation
page 167

REPEAT: 2–4 times, once or twice a day

5. Butterfly Stretch

page 155

REPEAT: 2–4 times, once or twice a day

6. Side-Lying Reach

page 156

REPEAT: 2–4 times on each side, once or twice a day

7. Full Body Stretch

page 164

REPEAT: 2–4 times, once or twice a day

8. Kneeling Spinal Rotation

page 166

REPEAT: 2–4 times on each side, once or twice a day

(continued)

This workout is for women who had a lumpectomy or mastectomy without reconstruction.

9. Overhead Clasped Hands Stretch

page 160

REPEAT: 2–4 times, once or twice a day

10. Chest Stretch

page 161

REPEAT: 2–4 times, once or twice a day

11. Walk a Narrow Path

page 149

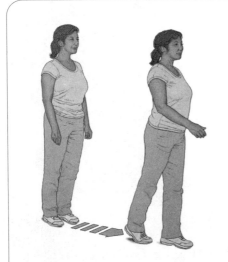

REPEAT: 2–4 times, once or twice a day

12. Braiding

page 150

REPEAT: 2–4 times, once or twice a day

Strength Workout 1

This workout is for women who had a lumpectomy or mastectomy without breast reconstruction.

1. Bent Over Row
page 177

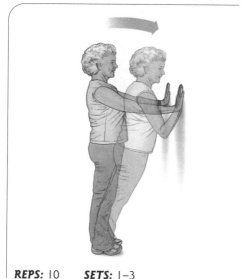

REPS: 10 on each side   **SETS:** 1–3

2. Wall Squats
page 190

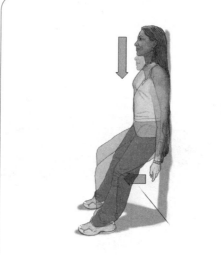

REPS: 10   **SETS:** 1–3

3. Wall Push-Up
page 182

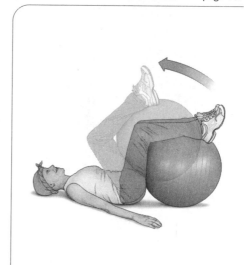

REPS: 10   **SETS:** 1–3

4. Reverse Curl with Ball
page 187

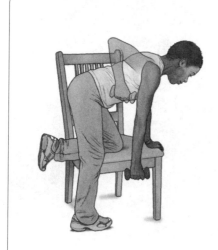

REPS: 10   **SETS:** 1–3

195

(continued)

This workout is for women who had a lumpectomy or mastectomy without reconstruction.

5. Bridge
page 189

REPS: 10   **SETS:** 1–3

6. Triceps Extension
page 178

REPS: 10   **SETS:** 1–3

7. Crunch with Leg Extended and Rotation
page 186

REPS: 10 on each side   **SETS:** 1–3

8. Pull Over
page 179

REPS: 10   **SETS:** 1–3

9. Opposite Arm and
Leg Raise

page 184

REPS: 10   **SETS:** 1–3

10. Biceps Curl

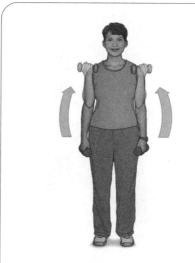

page 175

REPS: 10   **SETS:** 1–3

This workout is for women who had a lumpectomy or mastectomy without breast reconstruction.

1. Seated Row
page 176

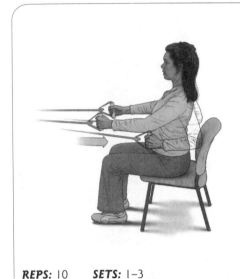

REPS: 10   **SETS:** 1–3

2. Wall Squats
page 190

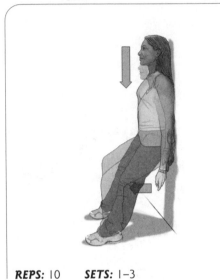

REPS: 10   **SETS:** 1–3

3. Wall Push-Up
page 182

REPS: 10   **SETS:** 1–3

4. Modified Side Bridge
page 188

REPS: 10 on each side   **SETS:** 1–3

5. Side-Lying External Shoulder Rotation

page 174

REPS: 10 with each arm **SETS:** 1–3

6. Bridge

page 189

REPS: 10 **SETS:** 1–3

7. Triceps Extension

page 178

REPS: 10 **SETS:** 1–3

8. Quadruped Transverse Abdominis

page 183

REPS: 10 **SETS:** 1–3

(continued)

This workout is for women who had a lumpectomy or mastectomy without reconstruction.

9. Standing External Shoulder Rotation
page 173

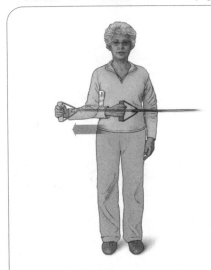

REPS: 10 with each arm   **SETS:** 1–3

10. Heel Raises
page 148

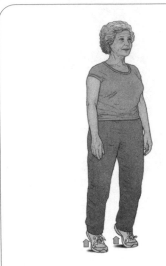

REPS: 10   **SETS:** 1–3

11. Biceps Curl
page 175

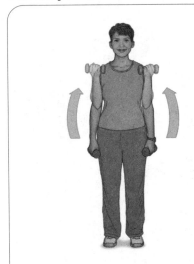

REPS: 10   **SETS:** 1–3

Balance and Stretches

1. Shoulder Circles
page 145

REPEAT: 10 times, once or twice a day

2. Wall Climb: Front
page 153

REPEAT: 2–4 times on each side, once or twice a day

3. Single Arm Wall Stretch
page 159

REPEAT: 2–4 times on each side, once or twice a day

4. Full Body Stretch
page 164

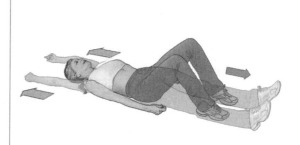

REPEAT: 2–4 times, once or twice a day

(continued)

5. *Butterfly Stretch*   page 155

REPEAT: 2–4 times, once or twice a day

6. *Supine Hamstring Stretch*   page 171

REPEAT: 2–4 times with each leg, once or twice a day

7. *Prone Press Up*   page 168

REPEAT: 2–4 times, once or twice a day

8. *Child's Pose with a Diagonal Reach*   page 158

REPEAT: 2–4 times on each side, once or twice a day

9. Chest Stretch

page 161

REPEAT: 2–4 times, once or twice a day

10. Seated Side Stretch

page 157

REPEAT: 2–4 times on each side, once or twice a day

11. Heel Raises

page 148

REPEAT: 2–4 times, once or twice a day

12. Single Leg Stance

page 151

REPEAT: 2–4 times on each leg, once or twice a day

1. Wall Push-Up
page 182

REPS: 10   **SETS:** 1–3

2. Wall Squats
page 190

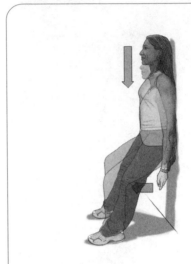

REPS: 10   **SETS:** 1–3

3. Standing Internal Shoulder Rotation
page 172

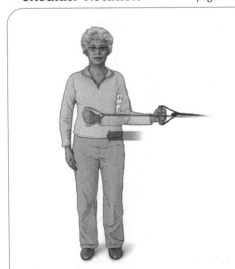

REPS: 10 with each arm   **SETS:** 1–3

4. Bridge
page 189

REPS: 10   **SETS:** 1–3

5. Side-Lying External Shoulder Rotation

page 174

REPS: 10 with each arm   **SETS:** 1–3

6. Reverse Curl with Ball

page 187

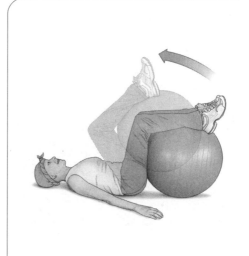

REPS: 10   **SETS:** 1–3

7. Triceps Extension

page 178

REPS: 10   **SETS:** 1–3

8. Crunch with Leg Extended and Rotation

page 186

REPS: 10 on each side   **SETS:** 1–3

(continued)

9. Opposite Arm and Leg Raise
page 184

REPS: 10   **SETS:** 1–3

10. Biceps Curl
page 175

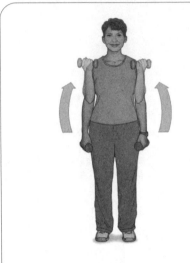

REPS: 10   **SETS:** 1–3

Strength Workout 2

1. Bent Over Row
page 177

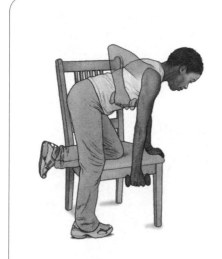

REPS: 10 on each side   **SETS:** 1–3

2. Wall Squats
page 190

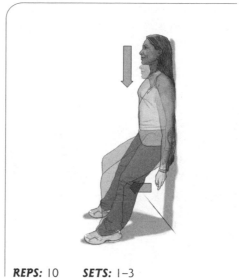

REPS: 10   **SETS:** 1–3

3. Wall Push-Up
page 182

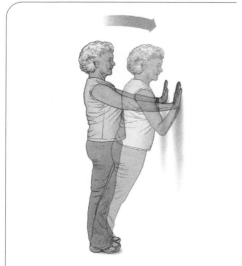

REPS: 10   **SETS:** 1–3

4. Modified Side Bridge
page 188

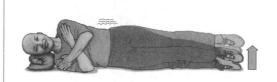

REPS: 10 on each side   **SETS:** 1–3

(continued)

5. Side-Lying External Shoulder Rotation
page 174

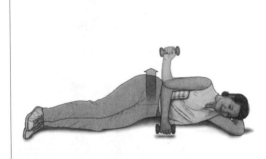

REPS: 10 with each arm   **SETS:** 1–3

6. Bridge
page 189

REPS: 10   **SETS:** 1–3

7. Back Fly
page 180

REPS: 10   **SETS:** 1–3

8. Oblique Press with Hand on Knee
page 185

REPS: 10 on each side   **SETS:** 1–3

9. Triceps Extension
page 178

REPS: 10   **SETS:** 1–3

10. Heel Raises
page 148

REPS: 10 times   **SETS:** 1–3

11. Biceps Curl
page 175

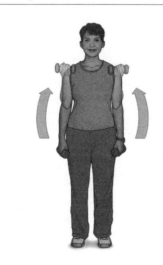

REPS: 10   **SETS:** 1–3

1. Single Arm Overhead Stretch
page 152

REPEAT: 2–4 times on each side, once or twice a day

2. Pelvic Tilt
page 147

REPEAT: 10 times, once or twice a day

3. Supine Stretch
page 163

REPEAT: 2–4 times, once or twice a day

4. Supine Hip Flexor Stretch
page 170

REPEAT: 2–4 times with each leg, once or twice a day

5. Full Body Stretch
page 164

REPEAT: 2–4 times, once or twice a day

6. Cat-Camel
page 165

REPEAT: 2–4 times, once or twice a day

7. Kneeling Hip Flexor Stretch
page 169

REPEAT: 2–4 times on each side, once or twice a day

8. Overhead Clasped Hands Stretch
page 160

REPEAT: 2–4 times, once or twice a day

(continued)

9. Single Arm Wall Stretch   page 159

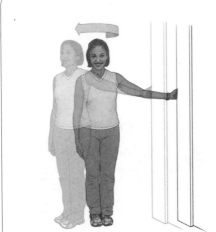

REPEAT: 2–4 times on each side, once or twice a day

10. Prone Press Up   page 168

REPEAT: 2–4 times, once or twice a day

11. Heel Raises   page 148

REPEAT: 2–4 times, once or twice a day

12. Single Leg Stance   page 151

REPEAT: 2–4 times on each leg, once or twice a day

Strength Workout 1

1. Seated Row
page 176

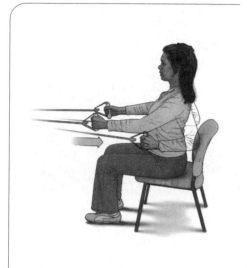

REPS: 10   **SETS:** 1–3

2. Wall Squats
page 190

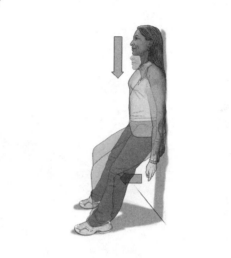

REPS: 10   **SETS:** 1–3

3. Wall Push-Up
page 182

REPS: 10   **SETS:** 1–3

4. Quadruped Transverse Abdominis
page 183

REPS: 10   **SETS:** 1–3

213

(continued)

5. Pull Over
page 179

REPS: 10   **SETS:** 1–3

6. Bridge
page 189

REPS: 10   **SETS:** 1–3

7. Triceps Extension
page 178

REPS: 10   **SETS:** 1–3

8. Reverse Curl with Ball
page 187

REPS: 10   **SETS:** 1–3

9. Opposite Arm and Leg Raise

page 184

REPS: 10   **SETS:** 1–3

10. Biceps Curl

page 175

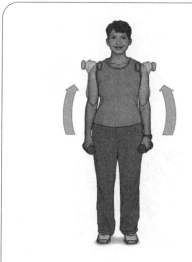

REPS: 10   **SETS:** 1–3

1. Bent Over Row
page 177

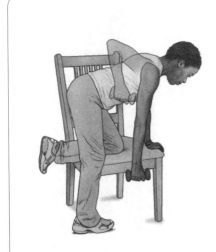

REPS: 10 on each side   **SETS:** 1–3

2. Wall Squats
page 190

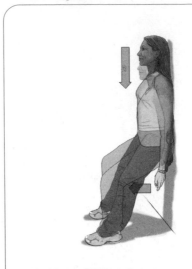

REPS: 10   **SETS:** 1–3

3. Standing External Shoulder Rotation
page 173

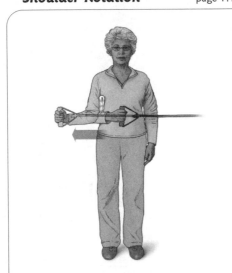

REPS: 10 with each arm   **SETS:** 1–3

4. Modified Side Bridge
page 188

REPS: 10 on each side   **SETS:** 1–3

5. Pull Over

page 179

REPS: 10   **SETS:** 1–3

6. Bridge

page 189

REPS: 10   **SETS:** 1–3

7. Crunch with Leg Extended and Rotation

page 186

REPS: 10 on each side   **SETS:** 1–3

8. Triceps Extension

page 178

REPS: 10   **SETS:** 1–3

217

(continued)

9. Opposite Arm and Leg Raise

page 184

REPS: 10   **SETS:** 1–3

10. Biceps Curl

page 175

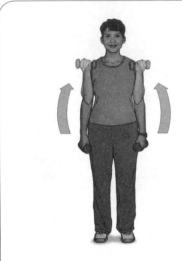

REPS: 10   **SETS:** 1–3

Balance and Stretches

1. Shoulder Pendulum
page 144

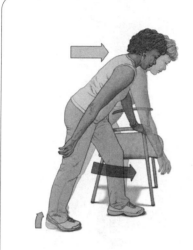

REPEAT: 10 times, once or twice a day

2. Wall Climb: Side
page 154

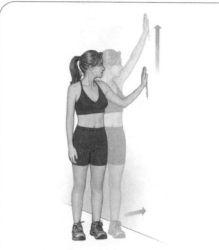

REPEAT: 2–4 times on each side, once or twice a day

3. Scapula Squeezes
page 146

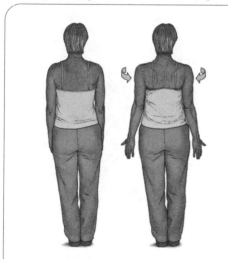

REPEAT: 10 times, once or twice a day

4. Overhead Clasped Hands Stretch
page 160

REPEAT: 2–4 times, once or twice a day

219

(continued)

5. Shoulder Stretch
page 162

REPEAT: 2–4 times on each side, once or twice a day

6. Chest Stretch
page 161

REPEAT: 2–4 times, once or twice a day

7. Side-Lying Reach
page 156

REPEAT: 2–4 times on each side, once or twice a day

8. Child's Pose with a Diagonal Reach
page 158

REPEAT: 2–4 times on each side, once or twice a day

9. Supine Torso Rotation   page 167

REPEAT: 2–4 times, once or twice a day

10. Kneeling Spinal Rotation   page 166

REPEAT: 2–4 times on each side, once or twice a day

11. Walk a Narrow Path   page 149

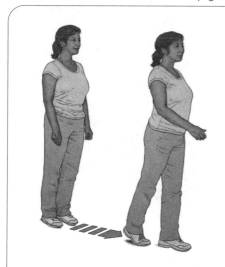

REPEAT: 2–4 times, once or twice a day

12. Braiding   page 150

REPEAT: 2–4 times, once or twice a day

1. SeNe Row page 176

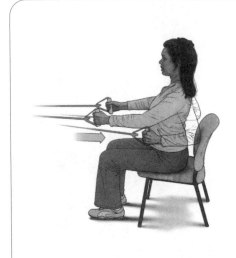

REPS: 10   ***SETS:*** 1–3

2. Wall Squats page 190

REPS: 10   ***SETS:*** 1–3

3. Wall Push-Up page 182

REPS: 10   ***SETS:*** 1–3

4. Crunch with Leg Extended and Rotation page 186

REPS: 10 on each side   ***SETS:*** 1–3

5. Pull Over
page 179

REPS: 10   **SETS:** 1–3

6. Modified Side Bridge
page 188

REPS: 10 on each side   **SETS:** 1–3

7. Triceps Extension
page 178

REPS: 10   **SETS:** 1–3

8. Opposite Arm and Leg Raise
page 184

REPS: 10   **SETS:** 1–3

223

(continued)

9. V Raise
page 181

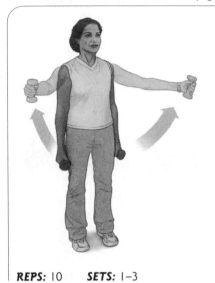

REPS: 10   **SETS:** 1–3

10. Heel Raises
page 148

REPS: 10   **SETS:** 1–3

11. Biceps Curl
page 175

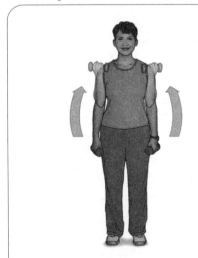

REPS: 10   **SETS:** 1–3

Strength Workout 2

1. Wall Push-Up
page 182

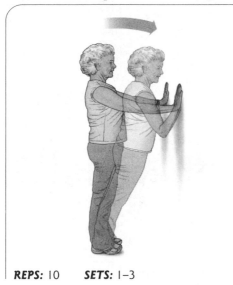

REPS: 10   **SETS:** 1–3

2. Wall Squats
page 190

REPS: 10   **SETS:** 1–3

3. Bent Over Row
page 177

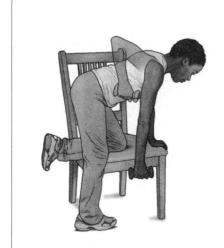

REPS: 10 on each side   **SETS:** 1–3

4. Oblique Press with Hand on Knee
page 185

REPS: 10 on each side   **SETS:** 1–3

225

(continued)

5. Side-Lying External Shoulder Rotation
page 174

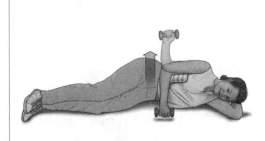

REPS: 10 with each arm   **SETS:** 1–3

6. Bridge
page 189

REPS: 10   **SETS:** 1–3

7. Pull Over
page 179

REPS: 10   **SETS:** 1–3

8. Opposite Arm and Leg Raise
page 184

REPS: 10   **SETS:** 1–3

9. Back Fly
page 180

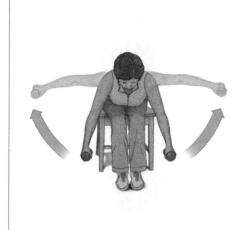

REPS: 10   **SETS:** 1–3

10. Single Leg Stance
page 151

REPS: 2–4 times on each leg   **SETS:** 1–3

11. Biceps Curl
page 175

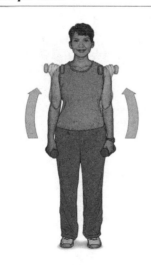

REPS: 10   **SETS:** 1–3

1. Standing Internal Shoulder Rotation

page 172

REPS: 10 with each arm   **SETS:** 1–2

2. Heel Raises

page 148

REPS: 10   **SETS:** 1–2

3. Standing External Shoulder Rotation

page 173

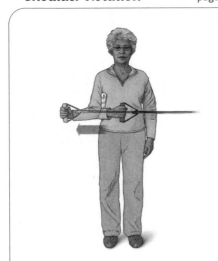

REPS: 10 with each arm   **SETS:** 1–2

4. Wall Squats

page 190

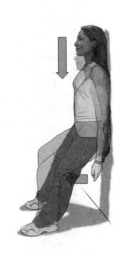

REPS: 10   **SETS:** 1–2

5. Biceps Curl

page 175

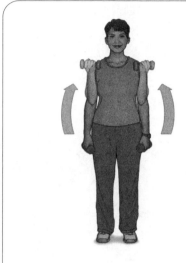

REPS: 10   **SETS:** 1–2

6. Pelvic Tilt

page 147

REPS: 10   **SETS:** 1–2

7. Side-Lying External Shoulder Rotation

page 174

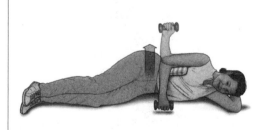

REPS: 10 with each arm   **SETS:** 1–2

8. Bridge

page 189

REPS: 10   **SETS:** 1–2

1. Seated Row
page 176

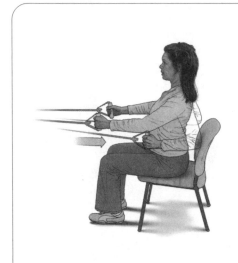

REPS: 10   **SETS:** 1–2

2. Wall Squats
page 190

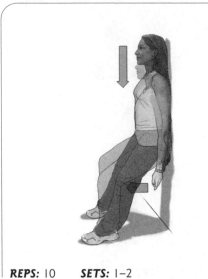

REPS: 10   **SETS:** 1–2

3. Bent Over Row
page 177

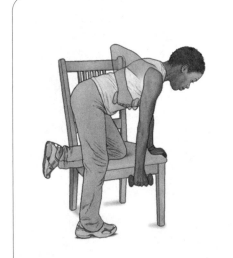

REPS: 10 with each arm   **SETS:** 1–2

4. Heel Raises
page 148

REPS: 10   **SETS:** 1–2

5. Reverse Curl with Ball

page 187

REPS: 10   **SETS:** 1–2

6. Bridge

page 189

REPS: 10   **SETS:** 1–2

7. Triceps Extension

page 178

REPS: 10   **SETS:** 1–2

8. Oblique Press with Hand on Knee

page 185

REPS: 10 on each side   **SETS:** 1–2

Resources

Websites

American Cancer Society
1599 Clifton NE
Atlanta, GA 30329
800-ACS-2345 (800-227-2345)
866-228-4327 (TTY)
cancer.org

American College of Sports Medicine
401 W. Michigan Street
Indianapolis, IN 46202-3233
317-637-9200
acsm.org

American Council on Exercise
4851 Paramount Drive
San Diego, CA 92123
800-825-3636
acefitness.org

American Massage Therapy Association
500 Davis Street, Suite 900
Evanston, IL 60201-4695
877-905-2700 (toll-free)
amtamassage.org

American Physical Therapy Association
1111 N. Fairfax Street
Alexandria, VA 22314-1488
800-999-APTA (800-999-2782)
www.apta.org

breastcancer.org
111 Forrest Avenue 1R
Narberth, PA 19072
610-664-1990
breastcancer.org

Lance Armstrong Foundation
P.O. Box 161150
Austin, TX 78716-1150
512-236-8820
laf.org

National Cancer Institute
9000 Rockville Pike
Bethesda, Maryland 20892
1-800-4-CANCER (1-800-422-6237)
cancer.gov

National Certification Board for Therapeutic Massage and
Bodywork
1901 S. Meyers Road, Suite 240
Oakbrook Terrace, IL 60181
800-296-0664
www.ncbtmb.com

National Coalition for Cancer Survivorship
1010 Wayne Avenue, Suite 770
Silver Springs, MD 20910
877-NCCS-YES (877-622-7937)
canceradvocacy.org

Susan G. Komen Breast Cancer Foundation
5005 LBJ Freeway, Suite 250
Dallas, TX 75244
800-IM-AWARE (800-462-9273)
komen.org

DVDs and Books

Breast Cancer Survivor's Guide to Fitness (DVD). Copies can be ordered through Brigham and Women's Hospital at brighamand womens.org/healthinfo/BreastCancerSurvivorsGuidetoFitness DVD.aspx. Or you can order through dynamixmusic.com.

Breast Surgery: A Guide for Patients and Families. Dana-Farber/Brigham and Women's Cancer Center. Free copies are available online through Brigham and Women's Hospital at brighamandwomens.org/publications/publications.aspx (see "Patient Education Brochures").

Eat, Drink and Be Healthy: The Harvard Medical School Guide to Healthy Eating. Walter C. Willett, M.D., with P. J. Skerrett. Revised edition. Free Press (2005).

Healing Mind, Healthy Woman: Using the Mind-Body Connection to Manage Stress and Take Control of Your Life. Alice D. Domar, Ph.D., and Henry Dreher. Delta (1996).

It's Not About the Bike: My Journey Back to Life. Lance Armstrong with Sally Jenkins. G. Putnam's Sons (2000).

Living Through Breast Cancer: What a Harvard Doctor and Survivor Wants You to Know about Getting the Best Care While Preserving Your Self-Image. Carolyn M. Kaelin, M.D., M.P.H., with Francesca Coltrera. McGraw-Hill (2005).

Mind Over Menopause: The Complete Mind/Body Approach to Coping with Menopause. Leslee Kagan, M.S., N.P., Bruce Kessel, M.D., and Herbert Benson, M.D. Free Press (2004).

Sally Edwards' Heart Zone Training. Sally Edwards. Adams Media Corporation (1996).

Show Me: A Photo Collection of Breast Cancer Survivors' Lumpec-tomies, Mastectomies, Reconstructions, and Thoughts on Body Image, 3rd edition. Presented by the Breast Cancer Support Group at Penn State Milton S. Hershey Medical Center (2005). Copies can be ordered through hmc.psu.edu/womens/showme.

Surgery Choices for Women with Early-Stage Breast Cancer. National Cancer Institute. cancer.gov/cancertopics/breast-cancer-surgery-choices or 800-4-CANCER (800-422-6237) for a free copy.

The Wellness Book: The Comprehensive Guide to Maintaining Health and Treating Stress-Related Illness. Herbert Benson, M.D., and Eileen M. Stuart, R.N., C.M.S. Fireside Books (1992).

Women's Strength Training Anatomy. Frederic Delavier. Human Kinetics Publishers (humankinetics.com or 800-747-4457) (2003).

Cancer Care Professionals

American Board of Medical Specialties
1007 Church Street, Suite 404
Evanston, IL 60201-5913
866-ASK ABMS (866-275-2267)
abms.org

American College of Radiation Oncology
5272 River Road
Bethesda, MD 20816
301-718-6515
www.acro.org

American College of Radiology
1891 Preston White Drive
Reston, VA 20191
703-648-8900
acr.org
Patient website: RadiologyInfo (sponsored by American College
of Radiology and Radiological Society of North America),
radiologyinfo.org

American College of Surgeons
633 N. St. Clair Street
Chicago, IL 60611-3211
800-621-4111
www.facs.org

American Psychosocial Oncology Society
2365 Hunters Way
Charlottesville, VA 22911
866-APOS-4-HELP (866-276-7443)
apos-society.org

American Society of Clinical Oncology
1900 Duke Street, Suite 200
Alexandria, VA 22314
703-299-0150
asco.org
Patient website: People Living with Cancer, plwc.org
(703-797-1914)

American Society of Plastic Surgeons
444 E. Algonquin Road
Arlington Heights, IL 60005
888-475-2784
plasticsurgery.org

Association of Oncology Social Workers
100 N. 20th Street, 4th floor
Philadelphia, PA 19103
215-599-6093
www.aosw.org

Lymphology Association of North America
P.O. Box 466
Wilmette, IL 60091
773-756-8971
clt-lana.org

National Cancer Institute Designated Cancer Centers
301-435-3848
www3.cancer.gov/cancercenters

National Lymphedema Network
Latham Square
1611 Telegraph Avenue, Suite 1111
Oakland, CA 94612-2138
Hotline: 800-541-3259 or 510-208-3200
lymphnet.org

Society of Surgical Oncology
85 W. Algonquin Road, Suite 550
Arlington Heights, IL 60005
847-427-1400
surgonc.org

Additional Support Information and Resources

Asian American Cancer Support Network
P.O. Box 2919
Sunnyvale, CA 94087
650-967-2305
aacsn.org

Mautner Project: The National Lesbian Health Organization
1707 L Street NW, Suite 230
Washington, DC 20036
866-MAUTNER (866-628-8637)
mautnerproject.org

Redes en Accion: National Latino Cancer Research Network
8207 Callaghan Road, Suite 110
San Antonio, TX 78230
210-348-0255
redesenaccion.org
saludenaccion.org

Native American Cancer Research
3022 S. Nova Road
Pine, CO 80470-7830
800-537-8295
natamcancer.org

Reach to Recovery (American Cancer Society)
800-ACS-2345 (800-227-2345)
cancer.org

Sisters Network, Inc.: A National African-American Breast
Cancer Survivorship Organization
8787 Woodway Drive, Suite 4206
Houston, TX 77063
866-781-1808
sistersnetworkinc.org

Wellness Community
919 18th Street NW, Suite 54
Washington, DC 20006
888-793-WELL (1-888-793-9355)
thewellnesscommunity.org

Young Survival Coalition
155 6th Avenue
New York, NY 10013
212-206-6610
youngsurvival.org

Activity Opportunities

American Cancer Society Adventure Weekend
800-ACS-2345 (800-227-2345)
cancer.org

Casting for Recovery
P.O. Box 1123
3952 Main Street
Manchester, VT 05254
888-553-3500
802-362-9181 (in Vermont)
castingforrecovery.org

Row As One Institute
P.O. Box 55
Newton, MA 02456
617-965-8806
rowasone.org

Team Survivor
1223 Wilshire Boulevard, Suite 570
Santa Monica, CA 90403
teamsurvivor.org

Protection from the Sun

Coolibar
2401 Edgewood Avenue South
Minneapolis, MN 55426
800-926-6509
coolibar.com

Solumbra (30+ SPF sun protective clothing)
Sun Precautions
2815 Wetmore Avenue
Everett, WA 98201
800-882-7860
sunprecautions.com

Index

Page numbers in italics refer to instructions for exercises.

Also by
DR. CAROLYN KAELIN

In addition to being a leading national breast cancer expert and a highly respected cancer surgeon, Dr. Carolyn Kaelin also is a breast cancer survivor. In *Living Through Breast Cancer* she draws upon her experiences as both doctor and patient to offer a priceless source of understanding, support, and guidance on coping with and beating breast cancer.

FROM HARVARD MEDICAL SCHOOL

Living Through Breast Cancer

What a Harvard doctor and survivor wants you to know about getting the best care while preserving your self-image

Carolyn M. Kaelin
M.D., M.P.H.

Director, Comprehensive Breast Health Center, Brigham and Women's Hospital

with
Francesca Coltrera

0-07-147880-9 • $16.95